*the
playboy
advisor*

THE
PLAYBOY
ADVISOR

Selected
by the editors of
PLAYBOY

A PLAYBOY POCKET BOOK

Illustrations by
Seymour Chwast

CONTENTS

PREFACE

Although many of the best magazine ideas are generated in flashes of editorial inspiration, *The Playboy Advisor* virtually created itself. Following the publication of PLAYBOY's first issue in December 1953, readers began requesting information about every imaginable aspect of manners and mores, from fashion, food and drink, hi-fi and sports cars to matters of taste, etiquette and dating. Obviously, the fusty, battle-axe perspectives being offered by Ann, Abby and their piously platitudinous sisters were found wanting by an increasingly curious and sophisticated generation of young men—and women.

From the beginning, each question received by PLAYBOY was carefully researched and personally answered by a distaff of one (lovely Janet Pilgrim), and eventually by a fully staffed Reader Service Department under Janet's direction. By 1960, with circulation exceeding 1,000,000, and the volume of inquiries averaging over 600 per month, it became evident that for every reader taking pen in hand, perhaps ten to a thousand were perplexed by the same query. It did not require a stroke of genius to realize that a monthly feature containing those questions and answers of greatest general interest would be an important—and entertaining—service to our readers.

First appearing in September 1960, *The Advisor*'s growth has paralleled the magazine's: Its volume of mail (over 2000 per month) has risen in proportion to PLAYBOY's spiraling circulation (now over 3,500,000); and its scope has broadened to cover a wider variety of subjects, just as PLAYBOY itself has deepened and diversified its content.

From the thousands of queries and answers that have

7

appeared in the magazine, we have chosen the most universal, pertinent, informative and—in our view—entertainingly instructive. Revealing and lively, this compendium of correspondence, we feel certain, will prove to be compelling reading for young, urbane men —and their sophisticated distaff companions—who seek both sane advice and delightful diversion.

—the editors of PLAYBOY

chases, conquests
and
mischances

chases, conquests
and
mischances

applying our experience
to understanding the distaff side,
we arrive at the following suggestions
for maximizing winnings and minimizing losses
when taking a chance on love.

I am 20 years old and am planning to move to Los Angeles soon. Recently I became close friends with a swinging chick who's quite a musician (I'm in theater myself), and she announced just yesterday that she proposes to go with me, to continue her studies there, after getting a job and getting settled in an apartment (with me). She even has $200 to contribute to the cause. Sound like a bachelor's dream? Not quite. The chick is only 15, old beyond her years in many ways, but nevertheless, 15. Is this or is this not bad news?— L. T., Bloomington, Indiana.

Bad news? It's the worst we've heard since our Aunt Matilda willed her millions to a Siamese cat. You may be in theater right now but you'll be in jail until you're

*old enough to play King Lear without make-up if you
don't act fast. Kiss Baby Doll goodbye and fold this
show before it goes on the road.*

Returning home on the train recently, I met a good-
looking young lady and we got into a discussion which
led to a few drinks. We parted at the station with the
idea of meeting again, but before I had a chance to
call her, she called me—that very night. She said she
was lonely and wanted to come over. Twenty minutes
later she arrived at my pad, toothbrush in hand. This
has been going on now and then for six months. In the
sack she's without peer, but conversationally she's a
real cipher. Now she's beginning to talk marriage, but
of course this is out of the question. Is there any way
I can preserve the *status quo*?—L. F., Montreal,
Quebec.

*Assuming you don't wish to keep the affair going
indefinitely, you can postpone the inevitable by keeping her mind off the subject of marriage. Most girls
like to think of themselves as Canadian Mounties, and
the illusion of a chase might keep her on the trail for
many more months. Bear in mind, though, that conflicting goals mean the relationship will eventually
dissolve. When that happens, take another train trip.*

I know for a fact that my girl spent a pretty wild
night with another guy she met at a party which I had
to leave because I had to catch a midnight flight for
a business conference in another city. I haven't asked
her for the details and I don't want to know them.
She is apologetic and reminds me that she offered to

11

come to the airport with me and that I told her to stay at the party and enjoy herself, but she doesn't reproach me with this. She just says it is proof of her devotion and that she misbehaved on impulse. Maybe so—but as I have pointed out to her, how can I be sure the same impulse won't overcome her again? She assures me it won't, but my doubts are further aroused by a recollection of how I first got together with her, a fact I haven't taxed her with.—H. V., Pittsburgh, Pennsylvania.

If your continuing the relationship depends on her fidelity, perhaps you should be warned not only by past experience but by this sagacious observation of La Rochefoucauld: "It is not so difficult to find a woman who has never been guilty of an indiscretion as to find a woman who has been guilty of but one."

I know you don't usually receive questions from girls, but I have a problem that I don't want to take to Ann or Abby. I'm 22, single, a college graduate with a good secretarial job, and I date a lot. That's my problem. Lately I've begun to suspect that the guys I date are interested in my body but not in me. I must confess that my figure is far, far above run of the mill, and I'm quite proud of it. I'm not averse to good times, but I think I have a lot to offer mentally as well as physically, and I wonder if there's any way I can be assured that the guys I date are really interested in me.—J. B., New York, New York.

Since your body accompanies you wherever you go, and since you can't conceal it or make it go away, it's unrealistic for you to ask your dates to ignore it. And, judging from your letter, we suspect your pride would be hurt if ever they did. A person of your attributes should have no trouble finding men who generously appreciate both your body and your mind, or a combination of the two, as circumstances warrant. And since you choose your own companions, the type of person you go out with reflects your own taste. If all your boyfriends come on like P. T. Barnum—"Every act an animal act"—it's as much your fault as theirs.

For two years I have been dating—on and off—a girl whose nose resembles that of a boxer. Behind that nose is a sweet, lovable, understanding human being. But the sight of that sniffer puts me off. Should I accept her as is, try to tell her in a nice way to somehow correct this defect, or simply forget her?— W. S., Chicago, Illinois.

To begin with, you can be sure she's as aware of her problem proboscis as you are. If she has indicated any interest or curiosity about cosmetic surgery then, by all means, encourage her in that direction, since the operation is relatively simple and inexpensive, facts she may not know and might be grateful to learn; fear born of ignorance may be all that's deterring her.

My girl and I are having fairly frequent flare-ups about dating others. I agree with her completely that if I do, she should be allowed to also. I agree with her intellectually, but not emotionally. My feelings are, bluntly, that I don't like it a bit. She says this is unfair and I say, "How right you are. I'm selfish and illogical. But I don't feel guilty when I'm dating other girls and I do feel unhappy when you're out with other guys, and you've told me you want me to be totally honest in our relationship." Et cetera. Then she cries or rants and I clam up and the evening is ruined. Last time it happened, I got mad enough to say, calmly and controlledly (or, as she puts it, coldly) that she could take it or leave it, we weren't married and had no obligations to keep seeing each other. My point was—and is—if I can't have the relationship on my terms, I'd rather do without it, though I'd far prefer to sustain it. Her point was—and is—that any third party would see things her way. As a third party, do you think she is right?—A. B., New York, New York.

No.

This may sound like a goofy problem, but it's got me bugged. I'm nuts about a new girl, but whenever I try to kiss her, her eyes cross as my face approaches hers, I bust out laughing, she gets teed off and the evening's ruined. What do you recommend?—S. J., Los Angeles, California.

Tell her to close her eyes before you lean over to kiss her, close your own, douse the light first—or do all three.

The girl I've been going with recently confessed to me that while she was in college she had several sexual experiences with another girl. Do you think this should make me reappraise our relationship?—M. M., Los Altos, California.

Assuming that she's kicked the habit, we think you've little cause for concern. Homosexual contacts among women are more common than is generally

*acknowledged; Kinsey's studies showed that almost
20 percent of all single, 25-year-old women had had
some homosexual contact, and the rate increased with
education level. One problem with such experiences
is the psychological scars they can leave. The fact that
your girl is willing to reveal openly her past experiences would seem to indicate that they've had little
or no effect on her present outlook—and this being
the case, they shouldn't affect yours either.*

The girl I've been going around with of late scores
an A in all departments—she's got brains, social savvy,
a pretty face and a terrific figure. But—believe it or
not—the latter is beginning to give me headaches.
The trouble is, she's very aware that she has a fabu-
lous body, and takes great pleasure in advertising it.
She wears skintight toreadors, form-fitting sheaths and
dresses with necklines that are practically illegal. Now,
no one admires the female torso more than I. Her
penchant for provocative garb is fine with me—when
we are alone. But I find it more than a little annoying
that when we step out together on the town she becomes the focal point for every male eye in sight. She
says she's just trying to make me proud of her. How
can I persuade her to dress more demurely without
sounding like a prude? Sure, I know—everyone should
have such problems —G. L., Chicago, Illinois.

*There is a bit of the exhibitionist in every woman,
which can cause occasional discomfiture in an involved
male. In your own display case, why not try a reverse
twist appeal to her vanity? Lard your conversation
with circumspect observations on the mystique of sex
appeal—explain that, to you, a truly alluring woman
is one who conveys mystery and a hint of the un-*

*known, who suggests her femininity rather than pro-
claims it, who, rather than spelling out the facts of
life, lets your imagination read between the lines. Try
to open her eyes to the difference between the chic and
the flamboyant—possibly by scanning a high-fashion
mag with her, or making admiring comments about
elegantly clad women in the places where you dine.
If the lass really does want you to be proud of her,
she will take the cue and package her goods more
modestly when in public. If not, we suggest you accept
the status quo, settle back and enjoy the scenery.
Everyone should indeed have such problems.*

A certain girl and I have been close friends for the
past five years. During this period the girl has gone
out with a number of different fellows, but not had
a serious affair with any until about a year and a half
ago. Then it happened: she fell deeply in love with a
guy who doesn't have a very promising future, and
who treated her badly at times. She had strong hopes
that they would marry, but then he got another girl
pregnant and married her instead. To make matters
worse, just before the romance went on the rocks the
girl was told by her parents that she is an adopted
child. As you can imagine, all of this had an adverse
effect on her. I now find myself falling in love with
her. But our relationship is in a twilight zone of mixed
friendship, love and retrogression. We are both persons with a defensive nature, she not declaring her
feelings because she does not want to be hurt again,
and I not declaring my feelings because I'm afraid of
making a mistake and losing her. I sense that she wants
to marry me someday, even though she hasn't said it.
The trouble is that when I show too much interest in

her she retreats, and when I act indifferently toward her she becomes aggressive—we just can't get together. For the past two weeks I've acted as though I hate her, but two nights ago we made love for the first time. Thinking that things were about to move forward, I have treated her with extra warmth since that night. Now she is moving away from me again. Just what do I do?—P. F., Phoenix, Arizona.

Treat her with all the tenderness you can muster. The girl has obviously been dealt two severe psychic wounds which will require time to heal. At the moment she fears committing herself to you (with the associated vulnerability) as much as she fears losing you. Confronted by your patience and gentle understanding, trust should grow, and the fear of emotional overexposure may gradually fade away. Although you don't ask, we can't in good conscience predict a successful marriage for the two of you and it would certainly be a mistake to marry until such time as the relationship is on a far sounder emotional relationship. Don't hope that marriage itself may somehow solve your emotional problems. It won't.

Is there really any such thing as an aphrodisiac? I mean *really*.—W. Y., St. Louis, Missouri.

From a medical standpoint, there certainly is. Cantharides (Spanish Fly), strychnine and testosterone (made from sarsaparilla root) are some drugs which are administered medically as aphrodisiacs. Their use is restricted by legislation in most countries of the Western world, and with good reason: indiscriminate use of cantharides may cause severe inflammation and extreme irritation of the genitalia, while strychnine is notorious as a torturously slow-acting poison, and the long-range effects of testosterone have not yet been determined. Medical aphrodisiacs are not new: for centuries, the Chinese have compounded an aphrodisiac drug from the ginseng root that is said to be extremely effective. It's when you get down to aphrodisiacs on a non-medical level that the areas of definition become a little vague. Generally speaking, an aphrodisiac is defined as a food or drink which stimulates sexual power as well as desire—contrary to the general belief that its role is only to arouse the libido, not fortify it. Aphrodisiacs may be employed in three ways: for their effect on oneself, or their effect on the object of desire, or both. So much for physiological fact; from here on out, we get into the area of opinion and interpretation. According to some, foods that are rich in phosphorus—seafood, for instance—have high aphrodisiac potential. Oriental bird's-nest soup is supposed to be an effective aphrodisiac because it's loaded with phosphorus. Over the centuries, there has hardly been an animal, vegetable or mineral for which aphrodisiac powers have not been claimed. Today, such disparate items as asparagus, onions, lobster, caviar, tripe, eggs, peaches, celery and spices (with garlic high on the list) are claimed to be aphrodisiac. Whether or not they are physiologically aphrodisiac doesn't matter too much: libido and sexual performance are so intimately linked to the mind that belief plays a major part in achieving results. Potable alcohol is considered an aphrodisiac because it relaxes the upper inhibitory centers and dulls critical faculties so that companions become convinced there have never been two more beautiful people. Danger lurks in the fact that after a certain point the drinker's performance will go down in direct proportion to libidinal feelings going up, i.e., the spirits are strong, the spirit is willing, the flesh is weak.

*Beyond that point, as many have learned to their rue,
things get too dreary to mention, and even the spirit
flags.*

The girl I've been dating for the past year usually
keeps me waiting some considerable time while she's
getting ready for our date. Over the past weeks her
stepmother, who is separated (and just 12 years older
than her stepdaughter), has become friendlier and
friendlier. Recently she suggested that I visit her one
evening when her stepdaughter is out with a girlfriend.
I have a good thing going with the girl, and wouldn't
like to hurt that relationship; but I find the mother as
attractive as the daughter and wonder if you think I
can burn my candle at both ends.—J. M., Pittsburgh,
Pennsylvania.

*If the girl ever learned you were having an affair
with her stepmother, it would not only hurt your
relationship, but would—in all likelihood—seriously
damage theirs as well. Stick with the daughter, and let
Mom make her own friends.*

Somehow, and I'm really not quite sure how, the
word has gotten around that my only goal in life is to
go to bed with the women I date. While I take a back
seat to no man in a healthy interest in the opposite
sex, my goaty reputation is really undeserved, yet I'm
stuck with it. I have recently become quite smitten
with a lovely lass but now find myself in the intolerable position of having my every word and move
misinterpreted. She reads a *double-entendre* into every
remark, a seduction into every innocent action. As a

19

result, there is an oppressive tension that I would dearly love to dispel. Do you have any suggestions? All pleadings of innocence on my part have failed.—R. T., Seattle, Washington.

Why not turn that albatross around your neck into an amulet? We suggest you make an earnest effort to live up to your advance publicity. It's obvious that your present liaison has reached an impasse in which you'll be damned if you do and damned if you don't, so by all means do. You may be pleasantly surprised to find that an amatory aura will draw some very attractive moths (even if not this particular one) to its flame.

I am a young woman who enjoys life and is not opposed to long-term affairs, or an occasional "roll in the hay," if the man appeals to me. But I do have a question that plagues me to the point of becoming a frustrating problem: How does a woman turn down a proposition from a man and spare his manly pride? I try to explain that the feeling must be mutual, and all men I've met agree that unless the woman enjoys sex, there is no pleasure for either. But some men persist, usually ending up with the accusation: "You're afraid of sex, aren't you?" So can you tell me, how does a woman say no and still keep a friend?—Miss N. H., Berkeley, California.

If a guy can't accept your straight-forward, level-headed reason for not wanting to go to bed with him without aiming countercharges at you, then we think you'd be better off losing this kind of "friend." Most men would understand and respect your wishes—and begin plotting ways to make you exercise your womanly prerogative to change your mind.

I've been seeing a girl fairly regularly who has all kinds of money. She's always giving me expensive gifts—gold cuff links, diamond studs, etc. The clincher was when she turned her Austin-Healey over to me. I've told her that her actions embarrass me and make me feel like a kept man. I've got a good job with an ad agency but it's still at the junior executive level and I can't reciprocate in kind just yet. She says doing these things makes her happy. I want to keep her happy but I don't know how long I can stay on the receiving end and still maintain my self-respect. What do you suggest?—N. K., Miami Beach, Florida.

Since you must think a lot of this girl, and, as she says, it does make her happy to do things for you, why not make the best of it and do all you can to return her material displays of affection with the kind of kindness and thoughtfulness that money can't buy? Besides, you can always think of her generosity as a contribution toward building the American economy and a sounder distribution of wealth. It's just this sort of conspicuous consumption that our leaders in Washington are plumping for. Do your share!

Two years ago when I was 19, I became enamored of a strikingly lithe beauty who was but a junior in high school. As our love flourished, so did our physical intimacies until, inevitably, our desire was consummated. During the next year our relationship withstood separations and the frustrating futility of long-distance phone calls. But the summer was marred by constant bickering and our time together consisted primarily of battles and bedtime. After she went off to college we drifted apart and, after one terrible Thanksgiving vacation together, we broke up. After two years of promises and agreements, I must say I enjoy my new freedom, but I am worried about one thing: the insistent urgency in our sexual relations. Now that she is seriously dating another, will she be predisposed to hop in bed with the next one—and the next? What responsibility do I share if ultimately she becomes a pro?—B. G., New York, New York.

Much as you'll hate to hear this, the answer is: none. The need for physical gratification is rarely the cause of a woman turning professional. What's troubling you is not her future, but your ego. It hurts you to think that you can be replaced. That's understandable, but what she does from now on is none of your business and certainly not your problem.

I've always been taught that if a fellow likes you enough he'll call first. Does this rule hold true even when a couple has had a heated argument?—Miss J. C., Buffalo, New York.

We think the rule you've been taught went out with jitterbugging; discard it. If the guy means something to you, pick up the phone and try to re-establish your connection.

I am bugged half out of my mind by a teasing young chick who is *not*, I am convinced, the usual kind who teases out of malice, unconscious hatred of men, self-ego building, power testing, sheer bitchery, or any of the other real or supposed psychological reasons. This is essentially a really nice girl who shares with me the firm, conviction that all my attempts toward mutual happiness have a shared basis in emotion, but she says that if I really "care" about her—instead of "merely wanting" her—I'll content myself with passionate goodnight kisses and dance-floor embraces. I've tried everything, including the lucidly sensible argument (to me) that "merely wanting" is just fine and doesn't demean or diminish her in the least. She counters my arguments with innumerable quotations from female advice-type columnists, all of which add up to "Don't do it girls, or you'll lose more than you can ever hope to gain." I'm fed up with these so-called authorities; have you got a counterauthority I can quote to her? (No point telling me what *you* think— she won't trust you as an unbiased source of wisdom, I'm sad to say.)—W. Q., Toledo, Ohio.

Try her with the following from the Reverend John Donne, he of the tolling bell:

> *"Who ever loves, if he do not propose*
> *The right true end of love, he's one that goes*
> *To sea for nothing but to make him sick."*

What's the best way of surreptitiously learning a new date's birthday, without questioning her relatives? —T. A., Clifton, New Jersey.

The horoscope ploy has no peer. Read aloud your own horoscoped future from a newspaper, playing it for laughs, then ask her birthday so you can do the same for her.

A girl whom I've been seeing fairly frequently is finely structured but somewhat lacking in gray matter. This bothers me not at all (her other attributes far outweigh her lack), except when we are in the

23

company of others. She insists on injecting a steady stream of grammatically mangled sentences. I don't think I'm a snob, but I must admit she embarrasses me when she makes such a display of her intellectual innocence. Is there anything I can do diplomatically to turn off my Miss Malaprop?—C. M., Dallas, Texas.

If she is as intellectually innocent as you say, don't try to muffle her; it will only inhibit the girl. Instead, play it for all it's worth. Create the impression that her garbled grammar is dizzily delightful; when she dethrones the King's English, laugh it up. Build her into a character straight out of Anita Loos—your own Carol Channing. Your friends will start seeing her in a new light. If Miss Information takes umbrage and decides to keep her mouth shut, your're still ahead of the game.

I met an attractive young thing at a party and, then and there, requested the pleasure of her company for an evening on the town the following week. She accepted. Seven days later, when I arrived at her apartment at the appointed hour, I discovered her arm in arm with another guy, ready to depart for that night out she'd promised me. When I mumbled my dissatisfaction, she announced that I should have confirmed our date by phone a day or two before the chosen night. Was she kidding?—J. L., Memphis, Tennessee.

Contemporary womanhood requires coddling. While we're not certain that women merit the vote, we do admit that it's often wise, in a tactical sense, to comply with at least some of the principles of protocol the lovely creatures establish. The creature you selected obvious insists on confirmation. Actually, we suggest you avoid making dates more than a week in advance; it's better to maintain a flexible schedule for those luscious late entries But if you do book well in advance, do confirm.

█ f you can give me a solution to this twist, you're wizards, indeed. I'm quite serious about the girl I'm dating, but recently developments have arisen to cause me some concern. "Developments" in the form of her brother, who just returned from the Army. Frankly, he's *gay, gay, gay,* if you dig. He makes no bones about squeezing my leg and giving me the "eyes" treatment when his sister isn't around. As soon as I realized what his angle was, I patiently told him I'm having none, thanks, and have done everything I can to steer clear of him. But he gets a big laugh out of it and says he'll have me before his big sister does. I've thought about slapping him around a bit, but any rough stuff and my girl is going to want to know why. —J. B., Juneau, Alaska.

Forget the fists—which is what he expects—and go straight to Sis with the problem. Since her brother's aberration now threatens her future with you, she has a right to know what's with him. Perhaps her influence can help steer him toward psychiatric help, which could give this fairy tale a happy ending.

█ fter many hours of brain-racking I've been unable to come up with a solution to a rather classic problem: Just how can I win back the affections of a girl I've been unfaithful to? Up until a couple of weeks ago our relationship was an extremely happy one. Then she left town briefly to visit relatives and I, being lonely and depressed, dropped by to see a friendly chick I used to date. There's no point in going into details—we had a couple of drinks, I made an automatic pass, and one thing led to the inevitable other. Unfortunately, word of this rendezvous got back to my girl. She was furious and demanded an explanation. I apologized, but how can one explain an act that was mechanical and essentially meaningless? I'm very much in love with her and would do anything to regain her respect and devotion. Any suggestions? —P. K., Phoenix, Arizona.

First, you'd better ask yourself whether this girl's "respect and devotion" are worth the price you may have to pay for them. If she is unwilling to forgive and forget an incident for which you seem sincerely sorry, what sort of relationship can you hope for in the future? If you decide the girl is worth giving up your masculine mobility for, then what is probably called for is a white lie. You've already been truthful and apologized for an incident for which you should certainly be forgiven. If she is emotionally incapable of accepting that apology, make up a befitting excuse for the incident that will satisfy her. If the girl cares at all for you, she will want to believe that nothing happened, so she will willingly accept even a very thin story that explains away the incident as a misunderstanding or something that never happened.

For the past four months I have been enjoying a warm relationship with an intelligent and vivacious young girl. Of late, however, my enthusiasm for her company has been dimmed by a desire on her part to "improve" my admittedly imperfect character. She has taken to proposing certain ground rules for my personal conduct: I should henceforth limit myself to a pair of pre-dinner cocktails, stop seasoning my conversation with salty expressions, and give up what she considers to be the bad habit of puffing a post-prandial cigar. The obvious thing to do, of course, is to tell her to shut up, but I am reluctant to risk losing the young lady because her approach to life is otherwise admirably emancipated. How can I straighten her out without alienating her affections?—W. F., Chicago, Illinois.

A woman's urge to purge her male of "bad" habits is primal and potent—but there is a way to curb it. We suggest that you explain to your inamorata as ominously as possible that your minor vices are merely emotional safety valves—and that if they are denied you, you won't be held responsible for the consequences. If this doesn't jar her out of her role as a one-woman reformation, try capitalizing on her sense of humor by quoting Oscar Wilde's incisive observation: "The only way a woman can ever reform a man is by boring him so completely that he loses all possible interest in life." Whatever you do, don't yield an inch to her wishes.

I've been going almost steadily with a girl who is an artists' model and who poses nude four nights a week for student groups in different parts of the city. Though I know it's unreasonable, I can't bring myself to accept the idea of all those guys drooling over her body. She says she thinks the world of me, but refuses to listen to my demands that she get other work. She says she likes posing—the hours are short, and the pay is good. Also, she says that none of the students have made so much as a pass at her. But even

27

if they were a choir of angels, I wouldn't want them staring at this chick every night. What's my move?— S. K., Brooklyn, New York.

We agree that your taking umbrage at her modeling is unreasonable; in addition, since the girl was presumably a model when you first met her, you have even less justification in asking her to give up her chosen means of earning a livelihood. You have two alternatives: Either accept the situation gracefully, or find a new girl who shares your sense of prudery.

A wonderful girl I have been dating has only one serious fault—self-deprecation. Whenever our conversation touches on a desirable quality of human nature, she immediately insists that she lacks that trait. Beauty, intelligence, popularity—she denies she has them. The fact is, she has them in abundance. Why does she do this? Is she a masochist, or is she downgrading her company through herself?—N. F., Labrador City, Newfoundland.

Your girl is probably just fishing for compliments with a variety of self-effacing hooks, a hobby common among females of all ages. If so, a little sincere flattery will help—the little creatures lap it up.

I consider my code of moral conduct about par, and am generally in possession of a clear conscience, but I need an objective suggestion for a course of action on the following: My best friend recently broke the news to me that he'd met the "girl of his dreams"— a beautiful, sweet kid, a wonderful conversationalist, etc.—and that they were making big plans for the future. We all got together for dinner one night and it seemed to me that his chick was sending off a warm glow in my direction. I put it down to the soft music and hard liquor. Several evenings later, I encountered same female, sans friend, decorating one of the swingingest bars in town. After a few drinks, she told me what dark, smoldering eyes I had and made me one of the frankest propositions I've ever received from an amateur. I declined politely at the time, but am now going through some soul-searching second thoughts on the subject. Should I have taken her up on it or told her to get lost? Should I wise up my friend or should I just keep quiet?—J. B., Chicago, Illinois.

Take her up on it, tell your friend, and let the chippies fall where they may.

For some time I've been making it with a very hip Scandinavian chick. She's everything one could ask for, but there's one problem: although she has fine manners and does very well in company, she can't resist trying to caress me in very intimate and obvious ways when we're in public. What should I do?— Z. P., Cambridge, Massachusetts.

Stay home, avoid crowds and get plenty of bed rest.

For two years I've been going out with one girl, and I have become quite dependent upon her (for dates and companionship, as well as sex), almost to the exclusion of all others. While she's certainly fond of me, I suspect I'm fonder of her. Lately she's begun taking me more and more for granted, a situation I'd naturally like to put a stop to. I've been thinking of scooting off to California for six weeks to "clear the air," so to speak, because I'm sure that after I'm gone for a while she'll come to appreciate me. However, she says that six weeks is all it would take for her to forget about me completely. I know you don't dig platitudes, but which do you subscribe to: "Out of sight, out of mind" or "Absence makes the heart grow fonder"?—K. O., Hingham, Massachusetts.

Platitudes we don't dig, but maxims we do. One of our favorites comes from La Rochefoucauld, who said: "Just as the wind will snuff out a candle or fan a fire, absence extinguishes small passions and increases great ones." Though you didn't ask us, we have a hunch you may be nurturing a very brief candle.

Is it ever advisable to physically chastise a woman who can't be controlled with words? I don't mean really hurting her, just an openhanded wallop across the rump, now and then. I'm not asking your estimate of the effectiveness of such action—I know from experience that it works. I'm asking, I guess, for advice on how to answer those who criticize me for it—including the current female recipient of my swinging salutes to her outbursts of childish waywardness, unreasonable tantrums and willful disobedience. (Being a gentleman, I hate to strike a woman, but she is better for it, and it may prove a long-term civilizing influence.)—J. W., New York, New York.

For an openhanded answer, we yield to other authorities: Oscar Wilde suggests that a woman should be struck regularly, like a gong; the Bible adjures her to turn the other cheek; and good ol' Charlie Brown says, "Never hit girls, shove them." Tell your critics to stick to their tatting or risk some lumps; tell your girl to bitch to Ann or Abby. (By the way, Muscles, since you say you're a gentleman, we're sure you won't mind telling us what caves are currently renting for in your area. Sorry—but we don't approve.)

My girl recently had a bad stork scare (that time of the month was a long, long time arriving); so much so that she now refuses to indulge at all. Do you have any suggestions for getting our relationship back to normal?—B. F., Arlington Heights, Illinois.

A misplaced period should not have caused undue alarm, provided proper precautions were taken. Apparently they weren't, and if this is the case, count yourself lucky and take a lesson from the experience. It should reassure your girl if you point out that, after all, the scare was baseless and that with the proper use of modern birth-control measures the chances of pregnancy are nil.

I have on my hands what I believe to be a classic reverse of the age-old problem of respect (or lack of same) toward women. Some months back I began to date a young lady whom I had known casually through family ties for many years. We got on very well—so well, in fact, that it was soon clear to me that we were in love. Finally, it was on one memorable night, things got started and before we knew what was what, the proverbial moment of truth was imminent. Summoning all my will power, I played the part of a perfect gentleman and, in what I thought to be a very diplomatic manner, ceased and desisted. Well that did it—on came the tears and the accusations that I thought she wasn't good enough for me. Despite all explanations about my honorable intentions, she stormed off in a huff and I haven't seen her since. Now I am beginning to hear through mutual friends that she has been saying that I am passive, a latent homo, that I couldn't make the grade with her, etc. I want to know what I did wrong. I mean, doesn't a girl want respect? Doesn't the gentleman's code count for anything?—D. P., Philadelphia, Pennsylvania.

You're getting exactly what you deserve. Rather than upholding any "gentleman's code," you've violated it by your humiliating refusal of the girl's ultimate gift. Next time around, try to remember that a gentleman may be defined as one who never needlessly inflicts pain or humiliation. People like you give chivalry a bad name. You can be grateful for this much, however: if the girl is now talking about the matter to friends, she is so insensitive that any meaningful relationship with her would have been impossible and probably would have ended in grief.

■ am a woman, 36, and all my life I have preferred the company of women to men. I have never regarded this as a problem—I have led a useful and productive life, and have never done anyone any intentional harm. There is a couple in my apartment house—I'll call them the Smiths. In the last few months, I have become very friendly with Mrs. Smith, if you know what I mean. I honestly thought that Mrs. Smith was one of those who also preferred the company of women, but who, like many of us, had chosen to marry. But now it turns out that she was not—that I was her first close woman friend. And most unbelievable of all, Mrs. Smith wants to leave her husband and move in with me. This is ridiculous. I never encouraged her that much. And she has three children to care for! I don't want her to leave her husband, much less move in with me. But this is what she insists she wants to do. I'm well established in business here and I am not about to leave town. But what else is there to do?—Miss N. D., San Francisco, California.

Having unplugged this dyke, and chanced washing up a marriage, you now casually survey the prospective wreckage. Whether Mrs. Smith was experienced in we-know-what-you-mean or not, you must have been aware that a five-member family was at stake when you indulged in your first flirtation with her. The affair having gone as far as it has, you should arrange to move to another part of town at once and make a point of avoiding further contact of any sort with Mrs. Smith in the future.

I've been steadying it with a beautiful chick for nearly two months now. But there's something missing from our relationship and I know exactly what it is. I've tried to get her up to my place but she fears the entrance of my roommates who are very good platonic friends of hers. (My roommates are big on platonic relationships.) Her house is virtually out of the question and I'm not one for car conquests. Also missing are friends with pads. So where do we go? —A. B., Cincinnati, Ohio.

To a pad of your own or to a less inhibited chick, that's where. We prefer the former solution because we feel there is no reason for either you or the girl to share your affair with your pals. If you can't solve the where-to problem, you'll never make it through the how-to stage.

Last spring and summer I had a successful affair with a girl I'll call Julia. During this time I became well acquainted with her sister, Jane, who is a couple of years younger and lives with her parents here in Austin. In the fall Julia went to Germany for a year of study. Judging from her letters, I feel certain there is strong mutual desire to resume the affair when she returns. A couple of weeks ago I needed a date and called Jane. We have seen each other several times since and I am now on second base with very good prospects of scoring soon. Last night I saw Jane and she said her sister has changed her mind and will be home in two weeks to stay for a month or more with her parents (and Jane). How can I share a pillow with Julia and still keep Jane warm for the future? Or, how can I share a pillow with Jane and not make Julia mad enough to upset the whole thing for Jane and me? Is there any way to solve this short of splitsville?—J. P., Austin, Texas.

Continuing your baseball analogy, your interest in turning this night game into a double-header is apt to cause you to be shut out in both; final score: no runs, no hits, two errors. Make up your mind which of the sisters you prefer and then act accordingly.

After being involved with a most charming and elegant young lady for three wonderful months, I'm becoming increasingly disturbed by her financial irresponsibility. First she wanted to borrow money to redecorate her apartment, a request that I gladly met. Then she borrowed money to buy two new, strikingly expensive dresses. And two or three times she has asked for a loan of $50 or so until her "dividend checks come in." As you've undoubtedly guessed, in not one instance have I received my money back. Up till now I have made no mention of the money to her, first because I don't want to give an impression of being petty, and second, I have quite frankly been afraid of disturbing or somehow disrupting the most successful physical relationship I have ever had with a woman. What bothers me most about the whole affair is that she is so obviously a young lady of good breeding and education. I guess I just didn't expect this sort of treatment from someone of her kind. What should I do? Am I—as I suspect—being played for a very large sucker?—T. D., Los Angeles, California.

Not at all—you've simply become a dues-paying member of the world's most venerable club. Whether you have been willing to face the fact previously or not, it is time you recognized that you are not spending your intimate moments with this aristocratic miss for free. So take stock on that more realistic basis, and, if she is worth financing as a part-time mistress, continue the relationship, but don't expect repayment in dollars and cents. If you don't consider her to be worth the price of admission, stop shelling out—and be fully prepared for a prompt, if perhaps regretful, alienation of her affections.

█ date a girl who lives with her parents and I get along with them well. Recently, when her dad was out of town on a business trip—which I now know to be a fairly frequent occurrence—I asked her to dinner and she asked if I didn't want to invite her mother to join us. Bluntly, I did not, but I said OK anyway. This has happened twice. How do I get out of it in the future? The mother is a nice enough woman, but I have little to say to her and her presence is inhibiting, and that's putting it mildly.—W. O., Los Angeles, California.

Skip the dinner dates when the old man's away, or try this: Tell the girl you'd like to have a nice, intimate dinner, just you two, and does she know which night her mother might have another social engagement. Or make the next occasion a double date —implying tactfully that Mom would be a fifth wheel. However you work it, pick up a small bouquet or box of bonbons on your way to the girl's house, as an impromptu gift for her mother. This gesture will convince mother and daughter of your thoughtful attentiveness and regard, and should establish the fact that there's nothing negative or hostile in your attitude.

campus, class
and
coeds

campus, class
and
coeds

these letters

originate from the halls of ivy;

characteristically, they're imbued

with a spirited awareness of virgin frontiers,

of fraternity and of student bodies.

Currently, I am a graduate student at a large Midwestern college and, frankly, more interested in chasing grades than skirts. I've always justified grade-grubbing on the grounds that a little sacrifice now could pave the way for the good life in later years. However, a coed I've been seeing (weekly) has suggested that I'm endangering my health as well as my psyche by hitting the books overzealously. I'd like to hear your thoughts.—J. L., Chicago, Illinois.

Only a doctor can tell you if your health is in danger. While we feel that the future benefits of self-improvement usually accrue through present sacrifice, and that such sacrifice—within limits—is justified, we also think that each individual must establish his own balance of work and play. Lest your scales shift too far in one direction, we offer this observation from Burton's "Anatomy of Melancholy":

> *Hard students are commonly troubled with gowts, catarrhs, rheums, cachexia, bradypepsia, bad eyes, stone; and collick, crudities, oppilations, vertigo, winds, consumptions and all such diseases as come by overmuch sitting: they are most part lean, dry, ill-colored . . . and all through immoderate pains and extraordinary studies.*

If pain persists, consult your girlfriend.

Next semester I know I will be given the opportunity of joining a fraternity here on campus and I am frankly in a quandary whether to go Greek or not. I don't need the fraternity as a social crutch; I've never had any trouble establishing contact with the opposite sex. But at my school, the Greeks have practically cornered the market on choice campus living accommodations, meals and almost everything else that makes campus life a little more enjoyable. My question is this: Do you think it's hypocritical of me to join simply because of the physical niceties a fraternity offers when I think that initiation practices are barbaric and silly and the whole brotherhood bit fairly cornball?—F. L., Los Angeles, California.

Yes, we think it's hypocritical. The desire to take advantage of the creature comforts offered is one thing, but cynically doing it while holding fraternities up to ridicule and scorn is another. If those are your beliefs, fine; but be man enough to adhere to them all the way down the line.

Our school uses the honor system for examinations. The other day I spotted a classmate cheating. My initial reaction was to act as though I'd seen nothing. But after the exam I took stock of the situation and realized that, since our exams are marked on the curve, by not reporting him I was probably lowering my grade and the grades of other people in the class who'd been trying to do their best without the benefit of "ponies." And yet, my eventual decision was not to report him, because I didn't want to be a fink. What think you—was I right in choosing to be a patsy rather than a stool pigeon?—D. F., Boston, Massachusetts.

Anyone who chooses to be a patsy deserves to be one. The ground rules for the honor system are very simple. If your cheating classmate won't abide by the rules, he should be tossed out of the game. He took his chances, knowing that the only way he could be caught was for a fellow test-taker to turn him in, and when you gamble you've got to accept the possibility of losing. You have been had by your schoolchum's belief (evidently well-founded in this instance) that the fear of the "informer" stigma was too deeply ingrained among his fellow classmen for him to be exposed.

Two friends and I decided to live off the campus this year and succeeded in leasing a fine basement pad. It was the perfect place to bring the local chicks and they really loved it. In fact, they love our cave so well, they now come in force—four and five at a time and at all hours of the day and night. These girls naturally think that three guys like us are helpless and they want to cook, clean and press everything—including us! So now our place is famous and we haven't got a moment to ourselves and are suffering scholastically as a result. We don't want to limit the girls to a timetable for visits since they'd probably blast off entirely. But how can we make them a bit more regular with their visits and actions without offending them? —L. H., Toronto, Ontario.

Don't tell them when they can come—tell them when they can't. Agree among yourselves on certain hours when your place will be off limits for outsiders and post a notice to that effect. The realization that they can't wander in at all hours will enhance your aura of mystery and add to your masculine appeal.

During the two years that I've been at Harvard I've read PLAYBOY faithfully and have become both a devotee of and an expert on living what may be termed the "playboy life." Only trouble is, I'm rapidly losing my hair and am likely to continue doing so. The embarrassment attendant to this situation makes me ask for advice—or at least wonder what your advice would be. How about it: Can one live a rewarding college social life while in the process of balding? Can this be accomplished through some conversational gambit, or through some attention-distracting or -manipulating technique? I'll be grateful for whatever light you can shed on this problem.—S. S., Cambridge, Massachusetts.

A man's physical appearance—his face and stature, as separated from his grooming and the way he dresses, which help project his personality—is one of the least-important factors in getting on well either personally or professionally. What counts is the inner image that a man has of himself and how he projects that image to those around him. Premature baldness will undoubt-

41

edly make you appear older than your years, but this can actually be turned to your advantage: The most desirable females these days seem to strongly favor older, more-mature males, so this gives you an added edge over fellows of your same age, if you develop the maturity to go along with your appearance; similarly, in business, the opinions of the older-looking man are more apt to be listened to and taken seriously. As the years pass, of course, the lack of hair will matter less and less, for a number of your compatriots will join you in the Brynner brigade. We have known many bald, short and physically unattractive men whose manner, style and personality put them head and shoulders above their contemporaries, who had hair, height and good looks, but very little else.

What can I do about a girl who has plans to marry me in the very near future? I feel the same way she does about marriage, but not about the date. I am still in college and naturally want to finish the year I have remaining. But I can't make her understand how impractical—financially and otherwise—it would be to marry now, and she insists that the date be set within the month (to keep the record straight, this is not a shotgun situation). I have strong feelings for the girl and would not like to lose her. Any suggestions?— B. B., Albany, New York.

It would be a mistake to marry this or any other girl before you complete your schooling and have made at least a meaningful first step toward establishing yourself in your chosen career. If this girl is unwilling to wait for you to first establish the firm academic and financial foundation upon which a good marriage is built, you should probably have some second thoughts

*about her suitability as a wife. In any working mar-
riage, the husband should have the final word and be
the ultimate authority; if at this stage of the game
she is giving you a hard time on a matter of practical
judgment, the contretemps may bode ill for the future.
More than her feelings are at stake here, and you
should look most carefully before you leap.*

This may seem like an idiot question—and you probably won't be able to answer it—but it's a matter that's
been bugging me for weeks. I was at a party with my
girl and two other college couples. We were sitting
around the fireplace and I said to my date something
inane like, "Be a doll and kiss me now, honey." The
other two guys looked at each other, smiling broadly,
and then one of them said, "Oh, be a fine girl, kiss me
right now, sweetheart!" And then they both burst into
gales of laughter. I was sort of miffed and said I
didn't see what was so funny. One of them repeated
this sentence and then said, "Well, you have to be a
science major to understand the joke." The other guy
agreed, and neither of them would explain. I was embarrassed and I dropped it, but it still puzzles me and
makes me, an arts major, feel square. What has science
got to do with it, if anything?—P. D., Ann Arbor,
Michigan.

*The phrase that was supposed to be so hilarious is
a memorizing device called a mnemonic: The initial
letters of the words are the alphabetical designations
of the relative temperatures of stars. Scientist and
sci-fi writer George Gamow invented this mnemonic,
and science writer Willy Ley pointed out its major
weakness: In normal speech, the sentence would probably be spoken in ascending order of heat, whereas*

the progression O, B, A, F, G, K, M, R, N, S is in descending order of stellar temperatures. We hope this sets your mind at rest—and that you got your kiss.

As an assistant professor of English at a women's college I've become more or less inured to the fact that girls often get crushes on those who lecture them. This professional detachment is due in part to the local rule that we must not indulge in unfraternal fraternization with our students. But this semester one of my classes happens to include an unusually attractive sophomore who follows my words with starry eyes and gives me secret—and provocative—smiles every time I glance in her direction. This girl appears to be more mature than the rest, and seems to know what she wants. I know that rules are rules, but aren't some made to be broken? Should I date her?—C. A., Boston, Massachusetts.

No. Giving personal instruction to this student body can only lead to trouble. In the first place, her sophomoric glances may be motivated more by a desire for a passing grade than for a pass. And even if she really does want to give you a tumble, the price you'll be paying isn't exactly hay: in addition to a rule, your career may also be broken. There's no point in jeopardizing your position for this particular chick—not when there are so many accommodating graduates around.

For the past year various members of our fraternity have been dating a very liberal-minded nymphomaniac. Now, one of our pledges is planning to marry her. Of the six men he has chosen for ushers, four have had affairs with the bride-to-be. Since we have no chance of stopping the bridegroom, we wonder if it would be socially acceptable to have these men in the wedding party?—R. C., Lakeland, Florida.

It would be socially acceptable—and highly desirable—for you, and other gossips around the fraternity house, to cease the sanctimonious snickering and let the couple choose their own entourage. Besides, this question of etiquette pales when compared to the problem of whether or not the groom is, at his callow age and station in life, mature enough to marry any girl. But that, too, is his business.

I have reached a regrettable impasse in my relations with an attractive coed I've been dating all semester. We have slept and showered together, but she has resolutely refused to "go all the way." I have four years of medical school standing between me and any matrimonial plans I might envision with her; and even though she seems content to continue things as they are, I fear my patience will soon run out. What do you suggest?—J. S., Troy, New York.

Unless you care for this girl so much you're willing to remain celibate with her for four more years, we suggest you let your patience do just that. If you continue this relationship through medical school, you may need a doctor.

I recently bought six shirts with collars that have stitched eyelets for a safety-type pin. A fraternity brother who claims he's an expert on fashion says that this is cornball in the extreme, and that his own custom-made shirts of this type (which I admit I admire) require that the pin be put right through the material, at a point dictated by the type of tie knot he's wearing; that is, Windsor or four-in-hand. My haberdasher says my friend is nuts. Who's right?—H. M., New Haven, Connecticut.

Either type is perfectly acceptable. However, although your stitched eyelets are a country mile from being cornball, your buddy's shirts do put him one-up statuswise: the pin-through-the-material system is found in more expensive shirtings where the quality of the cloth is such that frequent piercing of the fabric will not cause damage.

I am a young man studying at the University of Illinois, majoring in physics, and living at home with my father and an older sister. Although my relationship with my father has not quite reached the intolerable stage, we barely pass a day without engaging in at least one good, unhealthy argument. He pays the bills in return for my services in keeping up the house, and this obligation, coupled with our inability to get along, has been playing havoc with my grades; I'm on academic probation this semester in spite of a 135 I. Q. Now, I'm not just another adolescent puppy yelping for his daily paternal affection, but even a "damn-fool son"—to use my father's term of endearment—needs an occasional word of encouragement from those around him. Do you think it would be best for all concerned if I called it quits under his roof?—R. C., Chicago, Illinois.

Yes. A part-time job and student loan will help you pull through financially, and the vacation from each other's ruffled disposition will be good for both of you, after which you may be able to establish a happier father-son relationship based on your economic independence.

I am a sophomore at a small residential university. Though I'm known as a swinger, my reputation is based more on words than on deeds. This is my problem. I find that I get more sexual pleasure out of telling tales of sexual prowess than I do from the actual acts. Is there something wrong with me?—B. N., Tallahassee, Florida.

Yes. We suggest you seek psychiatric counsel. Besides shedding light on your hang-up, the doctor will make a great listener.

My fraternity house has acquired a tandem bicycle for two, provoking a minor argument over cycling protocol, which you can settle by telling us who gets on the bike first, the guy or the girl?—K. L., Atlanta, Georgia.

Etiquette must always give way to safety, which in this instance dictates that the guy take his seat first, to brace the bike firmly before his companion climbs aboard her seat.

I'm a sophomore at a Texas university. Recently I broke off relations with my steady of the past six months (no regrets on my part—I'd reached the saturation point in a number of areas) and now she's putting the knock on me all through the women's

47

dormitories by saying I'm the prize heel of the century. What can I do to shut her fat mouth?—B. J., Dallas, Texas.

Why bother? Whether through curiosity, the urge to reform men, or sheer feminine masochism, many women swarm to a guy with a bounder's reputation.

For reasons that would be self-evident if you saw me, I'd like to know if there is an operation that can be done to make a person's ears not stick straight out from the sides of his head.—J. L., Boston, Massachusetts.

Yes, there is, and we're told by doctors that it's neither very difficult nor very expensive. You had best check with a physician. Bear in mind, though, that Clark Gable was once told to do the same thing and decided not to.

My roommate and I are both upperclassmen in college. Having lived together in the same dormitory for the past two and a half years, we have become more than casually fond of each other, and have, frankly, had physical contacts, even though we both continue to date the campus coeds. Knowing your broad-minded views on matters sexual, we would like to have your opinion on the following: Do you think a continuance of this clandestine relationship bodes ill for the future?—L. G. and B. W., Chadron, Nebraska.

Yes. If you fellows have already decided to continue swinging from the other side, nothing we say will deter you—although we certainly mean to try, since our broad views on matters sexual do not include the advocacy of homosexuality. If your minds are still open, we think you should consider Kinsey's well-known statistic that 37 percent of the male population experience homosexual activity at some time in their lives, without necessarily becoming lifetime homosexuals. You are probably going through a phase common to postadolescence, a period in which sexuality is high and during which the combination of affection and proximity in an all-male environment (your dormitory) often leads to sexual involvement. These factors, combined with the fact that you have already spent two and a half years together in the same room, indicate that you've been giving temptation the upper hand. We suggest that you nullify these conditions, first by changing roommates, then by accelerating your coed dating until you're both firmly convinced that girls are not just soft boys.

Against my wishes and entreaties, a girl I've been dating flew up from Texas a few weekends ago to visit me. Her college got wind of this unauthorized trip and expelled her, and to lessen the impact on her parents she said the excursion was at my behest. Now her father is screaming for blood, even threatening legal action against me. The girl has endured enough already, and I somehow feel it wouldn't be very noble for me to apprise her father of the true facts in the case. What's my move?—B. M., Jr., Princeton, New Jersey.

Any girl who demeans the good name of a friend to save her own skin deserves what this one has received. We suggest you sit tight and wait for the father to act. If the storm blows over, you can taste the pious pleasure of having helped someone who didn't

49

deserve it. But if the father ever questions you directly, you must emulate Lincoln, who said that "truth is generally the best defense against slander."

I first began going with Susan when I was a sophomore in college. Like a fool, I bragged to my fraternity buddies about our lovemaking exploits. The more I went with Susan, however, the more I realized that this was not just a casual affair. Of course, I quickly stopped my boasting. Now, almost three years later, I'm thinking of asking her to marry me. If I do, I don't know how I'll be able to face my friends. Advice?—L. K., San Francisco, California.

We assume you've been facing them successfully over the last three years, and if so, marriage shouldn't change things. It's too bad that you permitted sophomoric braggadocio to get the better of discretion, but that was three years ago; chalk it up to youthful ego building and forget it—as your friends no doubt already have. If you've been going steady with this girl since then, anyone concerned enough to think about it will have long since concluded that yours is an intimate relationship anyway, no matter what you've said or not said.

A friend and I recently disagreed on a technical matter concerning a girl's loss of virginity. Would you say that more young women rupture their hymens accidentally (in gym classes, etc.), or during their first act of sexual intercourse?—J. D., Joplin, Missouri.

The majority of hymens are broken in the conventional way—that is, via sexual intercourse. Bicycle riding, doing splits, horseback riding and all the other athletics that have been blamed by blushing brides since time immemorial do not ordinarily rupture the membrane. This is not to say that a girl cannot lose her hymen through nonsexual means; only that most girls don't. By the way, it's only a small point, but females—like males—rarely lose their virginity; they give it away.

∎'ve been planning to enroll this fall at an all-male college, but now I'm not so sure. I've heard that isolation at a noncoed institution might adversely affect my hitherto robust sex life. Is this true?—L. B., Brownsville, Tennessee.

Hardly. With great biological foresight, the founders saw to it that virtually every men's college is near a similar institution for women. Even the most isolated college is close enough to civilization for weekend dates. However, if you feel you thrive under constant female attention, you'd better consider going coed.

◉ne of my girlfriends, currently in Spain, sent me a magnificent wineskin. I must confess I don't know the first thing about breaking it in or keeping it fresh. Can you help?—P. O., Wilmington, Delaware.

Glad to. Fill the wineskin (called a "bota" by the Spaniards) with inexpensive, expendable wine, let it settle for 48 hours, then empty the sack, discarding the wine. This will remove the excess tar with which the inside of the skin is coated to close its pores and make it wine-proof. The tar that's left in the skin will keep it from leaking without flavoring the con-

tents. *When you fill it with wine again, you're ready for the bullfights. (Two precautions: Don't fill a wineskin with anything but wine or water, and keep wine in it at all times. Soap or detergents will eat through the skin, and allowing it to stay empty may cause it to dry, crack and, consequently, leak.)*

I've inherited a fine old pocket watch and, for my own edification, can you tell me the correct manner to wear such a timepiece?—D. M., Northbrook, Illinois.

Pocket watches—which, incidentally, are enjoying a comeback—belong either in the trouser pocket designed specifically for them or in a vest pocket. If it's to be the watch pocket, use a fob or a slim chain. The chain may be hooked to a belt loop, or anchored in your righthand trouser pocket by your key ring. An antique chain makes the watch even more attractive when it's worn in the vest; you can tuck the fob through the buttonhole into the opposite vest pocket, and hang your ΦBK key on the chain.

My girl and I were called "The Inseparables" until her parents, worried about our getting too serious, shipped her off to the University of Miami. She left with tears in her eyes and we exchanged love letters every day. But after two months, her letters grew cold and she started bragging about all the wild parties she was going to. Then she told me she was interested in another guy. During her recent vacation at home, I gave her the ultimatum—me or the other guy. She said she was mixed up and couldn't give me an answer. After that, things got pretty bitter and I took my troubles out on a bottle. The next day I opened up my sports car on the New York State Thru-way. The car was in Sebring condition when I started and now it is ready to be junked. A few days later I broke down and called her and we both apologized, but for the rest of the vacation I felt like I was dating a platonic pal. How can I get her back to the way she used to be? I have a chance to go to Miami for a couple of weeks soon. Would this be a mistake?— S. S., Brooklyn, New York.

Yes, unless you want to go schlepping around after this chick for the rest of your life. You've told her how you feel and there's little else you can do. Let her come to you now. If she doesn't, she's not your pigeon. (And, considering your bird-brained drinking and driving displays, we don't know why she should be.)

For more than a year I have been dating a young man steadily and want to give him a blazer for his birthday. My parents think it's in poor taste for a girl to give clothing to a man, unless the two are married. Since I live with my parents, I feel I should accede to their wishes, but I would still like to hear your views.—S. P., Brockton, Massachusetts.

The box of candy for sweetheart went out with spats. Today it's entirely appropriate for a girl to gift sartorially.

Being an intellectual, my only concern in high school was academic activity. But now that I'm in college, I have discovered the female of the species.

53

Therein lies my problem: I don't know any sweet little nothings to say to girls. Perhaps you could supply me with a few such phrases that would enable me to master the fair sex.—G. C., Ann Arbor, Michigan.

Sure. One little nothing we've had a lot of luck with is $2x^2 - y^2 - 2x^2 + y^2 = 0$. *Another good one with less intellectual girls is that old reliable "three plus one, take away four." Actually, there are not pat formulas for mastering the fair sex. Our own playmates dislike idle chitchat and a "line," preferring, instead, sincerity and the discovery of mutual interests. A good way to get things started is to evidence considerable interest in your date by asking her about herself, about her ideas and attitudes on various subjects, etc. People are usually interested in those who show an interest in them and it will be doubly flattering to a girl's ego to have an intellectual seriously asking her for her opinion. As a scholar, you may recall a Latin proverb from Persius, which pretty well sums up the value of sweet little nothings: "De nihilo nihilum"—"From nothing comes nothing."*

When should one use the designations Jr., II and III?—V. C., Austin, Texas.

When a son's name is the same as that of the father, the title Jr. is placed after his name. When the father dies, the Jr. is dropped except where the father is well-known enough to make it advisable for the son to retain the Jr. for purposes of identification. When a boy is named after a grandfather or uncle he gets the designation II after his name. The third member of the family to use the same name becomes III.

gainful
employment
and
capital gains

gainful employment
and
capital gains

dame fortune can be

just as elusive—and just as pliable

as any other desirable female.

her conquest is not a simple matter,

but her favor is well worth the campaign.

here is some counsel on how to win her.

■ 've been out of college for two years and am now in a junior exec slot with a fair-sized public relations outfit. I figure that if I really put in the hours, do the weekend bit at the office and make myself available for work on a round-the-clock basis, I can build a solid foundation in the company which will give me a good running start up the executive ladder. *But,* my girl seems to resent every extra hour I put in on the job; she seems to think I care more for the career than for her. I've tried, but I just can't get the point across to her that these next few years could be the most crucial, businesswise, for me and I can't afford to fumble the ball. I believe I love the girl, but she's putting it on a "me or your job" basis, which is really unfair. How can I do my best for both?—S. S., Cleveland, Ohio.

If she is merely "your girl" of the moment, lay it on the line; it's your prerogative to structure your relationship and apportion your own time. Don't start out by issuing ultimatums, do strive to win her admiring (or at least respectful) understanding. If you feel the love you express has elements of the permanent, first coolly evaluate the implications for the future of her apparently stubborn blindness to the demands of your career and its importance to you, not only in terms of your getting ahead, but also relative to your personal job gratifications. You have, in her present attitude, a crystal-clear clue to possible conflicts to come and to possible egocentricity in her character. It is up to you to decide whether it is worth it to try to involve her in your career—as a way of winning her understanding. Face three facts before you decide on a course of action: (1) A domineering, competitive woman may lurk behind the façade of the "girl" of today. (2) Trying to share the job experience, as we suggested above, can lead to unwanted meddling, or to your becoming one of those bores who has to tell the little woman every day how he slew the saber-toothed tiger, so proceed in this matter with caution. (3) However she feels now, if you let her make you a clock watcher and a man who works solely to buy his leisure time, rather than because he's vitally and ambitiously interested in what he's doing, then the time will inevitably come when you fail to forge ahead —and she will predictably lose respect and admiration for you as an also-ran or a failure. Finally, if you can look ahead to having to deal with this girl on a strategic level, instead of spontaneously and openly, then there's something far deeper that's wrong about you two for each other than a mere temporary disagreement about the amount of time you devote to her. It's up to you to evaluate the total relationship. If she can't be content with your undivided attention after you complete a satisfying day's work, it might be best to forget her, or keep your association a casually romantic one.

I've been using a motor scooter to get to and from the office and it has suited my needs just fine. Now, however, I've been promoted out of my junior-junior executive status and I am wondering whether I ought to turn to some more dignified means of transportation—the scooter probably gives me a Joe College label.—D. B., Chicago, Illinois.

If the scooter is the answer to your transportation problem, stick with it. More and more, urban executives have turned to two-wheelers as a desirable means of cutting considerable time from portal-to-portal peregrinations.

I've been thinking seriously about a career in the clergy, since it can offer a number of obvious advantages: free house and car, good salary, short hours, community status, pleasant working conditions, social contacts, tax benefits and (important for me) draft exemption. My girl has criticized this ambition, saying it would be ridiculous, since I'm an agnostic. However, most of my contemporaries manage to work successfully as brokers or salesmen without having strong feelings about finance or marketing, and I'm sure I could be a success in the clergy without strong feelings about God. What do you think?—W. K., Louisville, Kentucky.

On the off-chance that you're not putting us on, we think you'd be most unwise to consider such a move. No normal person could enjoy a lifetime of hypocrisy —which is just what you're suggesting. Every person should "believe in" his job—at least to the extent of accepting its fundamental premises and subscribing to its basic aims. This is true of all jobs, and it's especially true in a calling as spiritually demanding as religion. Hopefully, the friends you mention have chosen their various jobs because they believe in them, and because they find in them a means by which they can profitably express their personalities and aspirations. No matter how attractive the fringe benefits might be, you could never find satisfaction in the career you propose, and we advise you to forget it.

If you guys can solve this one you're wizards indeed. I'm a young (32) junior exec in a medium-sized off–Mad Ave advertising agency. I have a fine job, with a good salary and a promising future. My boss has taken a shine to me, and frequently invites me to parties at his place. I enjoy the boss' friendship—and deem my attendance at these affairs vital to my future prospects with the firm. The problem is his wife. She's a little younger than I am, and some 25 years his junior. I noticed her giving me the eye several months ago, but thought nothing of it. Then, on the first evening the boss invited me, unaccompanied, for dinner, she was all over me the minute he left the room. I had to physically disengage her (gently, of course) and barely managed this before the boss returned with

59

the drinks. Since then I've been invited back twice for more of the same. Believe me, it's an ordeal, which her attractiveness only compounds. I'm not down on extracurricular activities, but this one gives me chills. Please tell me how I can turn this woman off (without offending her, of course, since she could kill my chances at work) so that my friendship with my employer, and my prospects for advancement, can continue to flourish.—J. S., New York, New York.

Next time the boss asks you over, tell him you have a date that night, and ask if you can bring her with you. Since a couple and a half is an odd number for dinner this request is reasonable enough. Then pick your favorite girl—one you know will get along with the boss—and make sure she stays on your arm all evening. Repeat this treatment as many different times as necessary. It shouldn't take too long for the wife to get the message, and it will keep her away from you until she does.

Having just been released from the service, I'm anxious to replenish my civilian wardrobe. Could you tell me just how many suits, sports jackets and slacks are considered essential to a young exec's needs?— J. J., St. Louis, Missouri.

While there are no hard and fast rules governing the components of a gentleman's wardrobe, you'd do well to suit yourself with the following fundamental attire that should more than adequately take care of your needs.

For cool or cold weather:
1 black suit with subdued stripes (business)
1 navy subdued check suit (business)
1 gray subdued plaid suit (business)

1 tweed suit (spectator sportswear and country weekends)
1 solid black suit (cocktail parties and nonformal dining)
1 lightweight dinner jacket (formal occasions)
1 subdued solid or tweed sports jacket (casual dress)
1 pr. light-gray slacks (casual dress)
1 pr. oxford-gray flannel slacks
For warm weather:
1 lightweight gray flannel suit (business)
1 dacron-and-worsted black pinstripe suit (business)
1 lightweight blue glen plaid suit (business)
1 striped seersucker sports jacket with cotton slacks (both business and casual activities)
1 batik sports jacket with dacron-and-worsted slacks (both business and casual activities)
1 lightweight dinner jacket (formal occasions)

To be truly well equipped in the toggery department, you should aim for the acquisition of eight business suits, two dark suits for evening wear, two sports jackets (one check and one stripe), one navy blazer, eight pairs of slacks and two dinner jackets.

Happily, I've got a nest egg tucked away that I'd like to hatch into something profitable by investing in the stock market. I'm pretty much of a tyro and I'm not quite sure how one goes about choosing a broker. Of course, I could use someone a friend recommends, but is there a more scientific approach than that?— R. Y., Detroit, Michigan.

There are assorted ground rules to help you line up a good broker, and acting on a friend's recommendation is among them—providing, of course, that the friend has a history of successful investment. A good broker should be ready, willing and able to supply factual information, to obtain opinions from his firm's analysts, to offer sound advice on basic investment procedures and, on request, on the buying and selling of specific issues; when orders are placed, he should be able to execute them promptly and efficiently. Of prime concern should be whether your man's firm operates exclusively as a broker, or is diversified into a number of areas—as a dealer, underwriter, commodities trader, etc. It is important, also, to know your man's background and previous experience, and the number of accounts he is handling for the firm; you want him to be able to have enough time to service your account properly. It would be wise, also, to find out what shares your broker personally owns; it might influence his recommendations. Ask for the firm's financial statement and samples of recommendations it has made in recent months. Then, even though you have major sums to invest, try your man out on a modest order. If the test turns out satisfactorily, then you can have him handle your complete portfolio with confidence.

In the light of the substantial sums that are often involved, it's amazing how many people give less thought to their choice of broker than they would in choosing an accountant to handle their tax returns.

have a drinking problem, but it's not quite what you'd imagine. I have lunch with my boss fairly frequently and he happens to be a three- or four-martini man who equates an ability to hold one's liquor with manliness, business success, aggressiveness, etc. The catch is that one prelunch cocktail dulls my faculties to the point where it's about all I can do to get through the rest of the workday without making an ass of myself. I have a feeling that if I spill it to my boss that I'm better off doing without, he's going to mark me no good, but I still hate to act muddleheaded in the afternoon. Any solution to my dilemma will be appreciated.—D. K., Houston, Texas.

Honesty, to coin a cliché, may be the best policy in this case. As tactfully as possible, explain to your boss that he has his choice—he can have a drinking partner and a half-day executive or he can accept your alcoholic allergy and have your clearheaded services on tap for a full workday.

I work in the purchasing department of a rather large corporation. Although my salary is fairly modest, I do have a position of responsibility, one in which I am called upon to recommend the awarding of a great deal of the company's business to outside contractors. Which brings me to my problem. The other day the vice-president of one of the contracting firms dropped by my office, inquired about a big contract his outfit was interested in landing, and then, after some verbal fencing back and forth, suggested (circumspectly, I must admit) that if his firm was awarded the contract, on which he felt his company had made an attractive bid (it had), and was well qualified to handle (it was), he'd let me in on a stock deal that would make me a lot of money on a small investment. I think my ethical standards are as high as the next man's, and I would no more take a business bribe than steal, but this seems to fall into a gray area which isn't covered by my personal code. First, as I said before, I'm sure the man's company will do a good job and the bid is a very reasonable one; in fact, I had already decided to recommend that they be awarded the contract before the V.P.'s recent visit. Second, should the man's offer really be construed as a bribe? There is no payoff involved; merely a tip on what he says is a sure thing. I'd love to make a stock killing but will I be compromising myself if I do?—K. M., Detroit, Michigan.

You certainly will. No amount of rationalizing will change the fact that the V.P.'s siren song was strictly "Here comes the Bribe." Tell the man to forget the stock tip; if his company deserves the contract on its own merit, by all means go ahead with your recommendation.

I'm thinking of pulling up stakes and making my career in one of this country's metropolises. Before I decide, could you tell me which United States cities have the largest ratio of women to men?—H. D. S., Blacksburg, Virginia.

Using the U.S. Census Bureau's 1960 standard for the United States—97 males to every 100 females—as a basis of comparison, you'll find that the ratios in this country's ten largest cities are favorable indeed: New York had only 91 males for every 100 females; Chicago, 95; Los Angeles, 93; Philadelphia, 92; Detroit, 95; Baltimore, 93; Houston, 95; Cleveland, 95; Washington, 88; and St. Louis, 87. Bear in mind that these figures reflect total male and female population, regardless of age or marital condition. We assume that what really interests you is which cities have the most action. On the basis of our own experience (and we're ignoring ratios in favor of the ease with which unattached women can be met), we'd give the nod to New York, Los Angeles and Washington.

When I was overseas, I married a Korean girl, and the few months we've been together back in the States, it's been absolutely great. The only trouble is, I'm a junor executive for a large corporation and, frankly, I've been a little apprehensive about letting any of my co-workers or superiors know I'm married to someone of a different race. I'm not ashamed of her, mind you; it's just that I think my chances for advancement might be hindered. Unfortunately, there's an important company social function coming up: I want to go, but I can't go stag. What to do?—R. B., Cleveland, Ohio.

If your corporation is so out of step with the times that your wife's race or nationality would impede your advancement, the sooner you know about it the better, so you can make your plans to move to a more enlightened firm. After all, you can't spend a lifetime hiding your wife from the people with whom you work, out of fear that they might not understand or approve. The best way to find out is to take your wife to that company social function; you may learn, happily, that your apprehensions are ill-founded.

I have a little money put aside for investment, but since the 1962 stock-market crash, I've been afraid to buy stock. I've heard a good many references to "futures" trading, but I must admit I don't really know what it's all about. Can you tell me what futures are, and whether they're safer than common stocks?—A. T., New Brunswick, New Jersey.

"Crash" is a rather harsh word to use to describe the May 1962 market decline. And in the stock market, what goes down almost invariably comes back up— as a glance at the recent string of records the averages

have chalked up should prove. Trading in futures you could lose your shirt in a hurry—or make a quick fortune. "Futures" is a term generally applied to agricultural staples (wheat, cotton and soybeans, to name a few) which are harvested during only a few months but are consumed at a relatively steady pace throughout the year. The cost of these goods is usually lower at harvesttime than in the off season, but notorious variables such as the weather, the economy, and government agricultural policy join forces with relatively unregulated sales conditions and low margin requirements to make the futures market a volatile one. Consequently, trading in futures is nowhere near as safe as investing in well-chosen common stocks. When you trade in futures, you agree to sell a stated quantity of goods on a certain date at a fixed price. If at the time you must deliver, you can buy these goods at a price lower than the price at which you agreed to sell, you can make a hefty profit. But if the market price is higher at that time, you'll learn the hard way that futures trading is a risky business.

At a large and uproarious party last summer, my wife and I swapped partners for a night with my boss and his wife. This exchange has continued intermittently since then, but my wife and I want out, even though the other two are still eager. How can I sever this arrangement without jeopardizing my job? —P. Y., Seattle, Washington.

If your boss has the authority to fire you, you can't. However, since you weren't hired to play musical beds, chances are he won't dismiss you for refusing to. In any event, the question is not how you break this off, but when. To which the answer is: the next time the boss proposes a switch. And whether he decides to fire you or not, we think you would be better off to look for another job, since it will be difficult for you to resume a normal employer-employee relationship after such sexual shenanigans.

At a recent fraternity bull session we were discussing fringe factors that might influence a man in selecting a career. One of the fraters said he was sure there were statistics on occupational longevity, that is, actuarial tables giving life expectancies in terms of occupation. None of us have been able to find anything of the sort, governmental, commercial or institutional. Can you tell us which of the white-collar, higher-income occupations has the longest life expectancy, which ones are average and which lowest?—B. W., Ann Arbor, Michigan.

While general surveys indicate that professional and managerial men live longest, no study detailing U.S. mortality by specific occupation has ever been made. It's our view that college men more worried about living long than living life to the full, aren't going to get much joy out of their alloted spans, whatever their lengths may be.

One of the employees assigned to my department is a good producer who, unfortunately, has no idea of how to dress properly. Not only is he consistently ignorant of current fashions in men's clothes, but he also comes to work in wrinkled and soiled apparel. As his direct supervisor, I feel obliged to bring this matter to his attention, but I have hesitated to approach him on a subject so personal for fear that I might destroy the friendly working relations we now enjoy. How can I inform him of his shortcomings without hurting his feelings?—R. L. C., Columbus, Ohio.

If it is important to this man's job that he be properly attired, then it's incumbent upon you, as his superior, to bring his sartorial shortcomings to his attention—tactfully, to be sure, but firmly. If his dress is unrelated to his work, and it just irritates you personally, try sending around a general memo, indicating that neat grooming is related to high office morale. He'll probably catch the hint.

Lately I've been seeing an exceptional girl who is a top executive secretary in a firm that directly competes with my own. We each enjoy our jobs and, naturally enough, we talk shop a lot. Now I'm trying to land an account that her boss is also going after in a big way. I'd like to know if you think I'm ethically justified in turning our late-evening conversation to this particular account, with a view toward picking up tidbits that might help me land this fat one for my firm.—H. W., San Francisco, California

What you're talking about is called spying in our book— and worst of all, you want to betray the confidence of someone who apparently likes and trusts you. Ethics aside, if your friend's really an "exceptional girl," she'll have sense and loyalty enough to keep her mouth shut when you start probing.

As a junior executive in a large, rather structured organization, I just found out through the office grapevine that my buddy, who holds a similar job to mine, is going to be fired within the month. I'd like to tip him off, but if I do, he's likely to make a scene with the boss and possibly give away my confidence. If I don't tell him, he may eventually find out I knew and think me a fink. What do I do?—A. J., Dallas, Texas.

We think mum's the word. Your first consideration ought to be that the grapevine might be producing sour wine. Conceivably, you could convey false scuttlebutt to your friend, who, on the basis of it, might make a fool of himself and thus get fired. If the information is indeed correct, then your telling him will not alter it.

I 've talked with several different friends about this problem and have heard different opinions. I'm a sales trainee and my desk is arranged so as to keep anyone I'm talking with from getting within four feet of me. Often I feel that this distance sets up a physical barrier which is actually harmful to sales. Is there any proper distance which should separate two men in a business discussion?—A. L., Hartford, Connecticut.

The proper distance is the one most comfortable for you. Rearrange your office so you can get closer to your customers, but leave them room for retreat. Most English-speaking businessmen seem to prefer conversation over the impersonal expanse of a desk top, while Spanish speakers will generally climb all over such barricades to achieve a closer discussion.

T he firm in which I'm a secretary is short on bachelors. More than once I've turned down luncheon invitations from married male co-workers, because I feared unnecessary gossip. Do you think it's acceptable for a single woman to lunch with a married man?— R. D., Los Angeles, California.

"Acceptable," yes; whether several luncheons with the same married male might not lead to presumably unwelcome emotional involvement, on one or both parts, is another matter. If you wish to avoid that possibility, but enjoy masculine company when you dine, the best solution is to try to arrange for a group of several co-workers, both male and female, to lunch together.

I have some money invested in mutual funds, and was surprised when a broker friend of mine told me that mutual funds have been faring worse than the common stock averages. Is this true? Which in your opinion, make the better investment—mutual funds or common stocks?—K. J., Milwaukee, Wisconsin.

It's true that the combined growth rate of all mutual funds (mutual funds are investment companies that buy and own stock in many different corporations) has in the past two or three years been outstripped by the pace of most accepted stock averages. What this observation doesn't consider is that no reasonable investor would limit his purchases to an equal sampling of (for instance) the 30 blue-chip stocks that comprise the Dow Jones Industrial Stock Average, any more than he would deploy his money equally among all mutual funds. Most mutual funds invest conservatively (to provide liberal income and security), so their very nature makes rapid price appreciation unlikely. Many funds successfully imitate the characteristics of individual common stocks, offering such diverse in-

vestment objectives as rapid growth, high income or blue-chip saefty. The rub is that these special-purpose funds will never fare better than the individual stocks that comprise them—stocks which the savvy investor could buy himself without paying mutual fund commissions. When all is said and done, whether you should invest in mutual funds or common stocks depends mainly on your own income and financial habits. If you have neither the time nor the inclination to read the market pages every day, and if your tax bracket is at a level where the prospect of additional taxable income doesn't dismay you (say, under $20,000), then mutual funds are probably your best bet. However, if you enjoy The Wall Street Journal and have time to follow the market, or if your income is large enough to justify experiments in the 20th Century alchemy of capital gains, then you may be better off investing in common stocks

Several years ago, when I was just out of the Army and sorely in need of work, I hoked up a résumé and invented an impressive past in order to secure a job for which my real credentials wouldn't qualify me. As it turned out, I was hired, and since then I've been quite successful in my work—so much that another firm is considering me for a much better position. The problem is this: In my years here I've had to maintain the false past which landed me my job in the first place. This fabrication has become more and more annoying as I've advanced on my own real merits. I'd like to be rid of it once and for all.

In a few weeks I'm scheduled for a thorough interview for a responsible executive position with an important manufacturing company. Do you think I should reveal the truth about my background—which includes the fact that I only completed three years of college?—K. H., St. Louis, Missouri.

By all means. Proven ability of the sort you've evidenced in your current job is far more important than your biographical background. If you continue living a lie, the chances are that sooner or later you'll be exposed—and a history of falsifying employment information would be much more harmful to your career than the mere lack of a college diploma. Tell your new employer the whole truth and nothing but the truth.

Is it correct to wear loafers with a business suit? I've seen a number of executives whom I could classify as well-dressed sporting them about the office.—T. T., Seattle, Washington.

It isn't, if you mean the classic moccasin-styled loafer, which should be confined to more casual attire. But there are much more formal versions—slip-ons—which are perfectly acceptable with a business suit.

Are there any disadvantages in putting your money in a savings-and-loan association rather than in a savings bank, since both are insured and savings-and-loan associations generally offer higher interest rates than savings banks?—L. K., San Diego, California.

The one disadvantage is in the type of insurance. The Federal Deposit Insurance Corporation, covering savings-bank accounts, provides for immediate repayment or within a certain period upon demand; the

*Federal Savings and Loan Insurance Corporation's
coverage doesn't go into effect until the association
legally has been declared in default—a procedure
which could take considerable time.*

█ 'm a junior, junior executive in a rather large corporation. I have a yen to grow a beard, but, in casing
the executive echelons, I note a conspicuous absence
of chin shrubbery. Will I be put down as an oddball,
and will my chances of advancement be jeopardized
if I go the beard route?—C. S., Detroit, Michigan.

*If your job is one involving outside business con-
tacts, forget the foliage; most companies frown on
beards as an unnecessary handicap in dealing with
people whose prejudices are not a known quantity.
But even if your job involves only contact with your
employers and fellow employees, we suggest that you
place a moratorium on building up a beaver until
you've advanced out of the junior, junior class. By the
time you reach a slightly higher stratum, your abilities (as well as your personality and personal habits)
will be better known; then you can grow a beard with
impunity and join the estimable ranks of Commander
Whitehead, Peter Ustinov, Jim Moran, Skitch Hen-
derson, John Steinbeck and PLAYBOY's own Shel
Silverstein.*

█ 've been thinking of switching to pipes, because I've
heard that the pipe smoker is more likely to land a
better job, because he looks wiser, more self-assured,
more mature and is a good bet to live longer. I'm 22,
just starting out, and want to have as many things

73

working for me as possible. Do you think I should switch?—P. S., Fayetteville, Arkansas.

There are several reasons why you might consider switching to pipes. If you enjoy a pipe, if you feel that pipes minimize dangers to health, or if you're just in the mood for a change, then switch. As far as impressions go, what you smoke is much less important than how you smoke, but neither should affect your employment prospects. As a matter of fact, H. L. Mencken once facetiously advised against employing pipe smokers, since, he said, they're much too busy puttering with their pipes to get anything else done.

█ never bought on time, never purchased what I couldn't afford, and always paid cash. That's my problem now. I've just moved to a fine job in a new city, and would like to embark on a life that befits my new-found economic status. However, I find myself totally unable to secure needed credit, because my pay-as-you-go past left no one to vouch for me. Do you have any suggestions?—Y. L., Shreveport, Louisiana.

The simplest way for you to quickly establish credit is to get a bank loan (a collateral loan, secured by your auto or other possessions, would be cheapest), put the money in a savings account where it will draw interest, then repay the loan promptly when it's due. This way you can immediately show potential creditors a nice nest egg, and after you've paid the loan promptly, the lender will gladly supply future cash and a credit reference to boot. (And while you've got a bank balance, cite it as you apply for half-a-dozen special- and general-purpose credit cards—useful credit devices, even if you never have occasion to use them.) If you shop around, you should be able to borrow at six percent and bank at four-and-a-half, for a net cost of a bargain-basement one-and-a-half percent.

When you receive a business letter from a woman and it doesn't say whether she's a Miss or a Mrs., what's the proper form of reply?—G. K., Boston, Massachusetts.

Unless you know otherwise—"Miss" is the proper form.

I'm a junior exec in a large corporation. For the past six months my immediate superior has been dating a ravishing chick who is unquestionably the most provocative girl I have seen in a lifetime of attentive observation. What's more, I know she's attracted to me—her smiles have R.S.V.P. written all over them. I'm itching to ask her out—but naturally I don't want to jeopardize my job or chances of promotion. Is there any solution to this dilemma?—L. H., Chicago, Illinois.

The simplest and safest course is to forget this chick and find solace elsewhere—bearing in mind that old saw about forbidden fruit, and that the world abounds in lovely lasses. However, if you aren't bothered by a bit of Machiavellian scheming, you might try this: Go to your superior's own immediate superior and pose the problem to him in man-to-man fashion. He may greet your confidences coldly; chances are excellent, however, that he will agree that office status should not cripple one's private love life. This resolved, strike up an immediate liaison with the doll in question. When your overseer learns of your

75

out-of-office activities, as he inevitably will, he will respond in either of two ways: he'll either accept the situation or attempt to exact revenge by criticizing your work. If he does try to stab your back with a figurative knife, remember that you have a powerful ally—his superior—who can assess his motives for what they really are: the sour grapes of wrath. Who knows, you may not only get the girl, but a spot promotion as well.

What are the advantages and disadvantages of buying preferred stock?—M. A., Jr., St. Louis, Missouri.

Owners of preferred stock get preferential treatment over common stockholders in that they have prior claim against the assets of the company in case of liquidation, and have the right to receive a fixed dividend before any dividends are paid to owners of the common. On the other hand, preferred stockholders generally have no voting privileges in company affairs, and usually won't get more than the stipulated dividend even if the company becomes a top bonanza.

A group of guys in the office on the same executive level have lunch together every day. There are six of us and it seems to be taken for granted by one and all that there is an open invitation to lunch extended to everybody. What I'm getting at is that I occasionally don't feel like lunching with a full crew—after a while, you get to feel as though you're at a board meeting. I'd like to break this thing down into smaller groups, but don't quite know how to go about it. I don't want to slight anyone, yet I think I'd feel silly making the suggestion about diversification to the group. What's the best way out?—S. H., Philadelphia, Pennsylvania.

We suggest you take your dilemma by the horns and start asking one of your associates at a time to join you for lunch. Pick out restaurants that are a bit off the beaten track, so there'll be little chance of bumping into the rest of the group. This should make the fact that you don't dig the mass mess as S.O.P. clear enough to the others.

T he man who can write out a check for his car on the spot seems to have a bargaining advantage over one who has to arrange financing. However, my own bank account isn't quite that healthy. I wonder if it would be possible for me to get a loan from my bank before I actually went out to dicker for a car? Would the bank be likely to go for this kind of deal, if my credit rating was good? If not, what kind of course would you advise me to pursue in this situation?—B. S., Austin, Texas.

We think you're wise in not wishing to buy a car on "easy payments" from the auto company—you'll get a better shake from your bank. But you don't need the full purchase price in your checking account in order to negotiate successfully. You can get a loan approved in advance, make any kind of deal you want with the auto seller, leave him a small deposit (not to exceed $100) and then get your money from the bank.

M y dilemma concerns a new job to which I looked forward, but which has put me in a position that's causing much anxiety and loss of sleep. I took this job on the branch-office sales force of a fast-growing company, after intensive interviews in the home office. Everything seemed fine at first: nice guys to work with, nifty offices, a hail-fellow-well-met branch manager of sales. Now, only two weeks later, I find that there is a tacit goof-off conspiracy. The company is doing so well that a certain amount of business comes in over the transom, so to speak. "If nobody works too hard, the general average will look good enough," seems to be the idea, and meanwhile the rule is long, wet, expense-account lunches and take it easy or you'll spoil it for everybody. The manager seems to be the worst of all: he OKs the expense accounts, winks at the loafing, often gets stoned at lunch and takes the afternoon off. I kept quiet and kept my nose clean for two weeks, then decided I don't like the setup at all, for several reasons. First, I want to get ahead, not just get by. Second, I like to be interested in the work I spend most of my waking day doing. Third, I don't like to sound stuffy, but—damnit—it offends my sense of fair play. Fourth, and perhaps most practically pressing, I'm convinced it can't last: sooner or later, the home office is bound to get wise. I have debated going over the manager's head, directly to his home-office boss, either by confidential memo, in person over a weekend (at my own expense), or even by mail, anonymously. So far, I've done nothing but worry. Sure as hell, when the whatzis hits the fan, we'll get fired. What do you advise?—P. R., Cleveland, Ohio.

The first thing we advise is to make absolutely sure your short tenure in the organization hasn't precluded your getting the full picture. If you're certain that the branch office supports a slew of sluggards, your course is clear. Don't try the over-the-manager's-head or anonymous-letter bit. Just do the best job of which you're capable and don't worry about antagonizing your confreres. They may be your friends but they're also your competition. Do a good enough job and it's bound to be noticed by those upstairs; if heads are eventually chopped, most certainly yours won't be one of them. If it is, then the organization isn't the kind you should be working for in the first place.

I like to wear a scarf, but I'm afraid it makes me appear senescent. What sort of scarf can a young man best wear with overcoat and business suits?— V. M., Arlington, Virginia.

There's nothing geriatric about a scarf—in fact, it's a smart and sensible piece of winterwear. A wool or cashmere scarf, preferably in some solid neutral tone, best complements the business suit. For an added fashion fillip, try a reversible model: silk on one side, cashmere on the other.

I will be moving from New York to Chicago, in connection with a new job, next July. Never having moved out of the state before, a couple of questions about the transportation of my household goods occur to me. First, how do I get the best price? (In New York intracity moving, some companies charge you by the hour, others give you a flat rate—it's not easy to decide which will come out better.) Next, I wonder whether to tip the movers when the job is completed. If so, how much?—I. F., New York, New York.

We think it's a good idea to have at least three movers compete for your job. This way, you can best learn what is involved, and can decide which company seems most reliable. You'll find, however, that household moves across state lines are rigidly controlled by the Interstate Commerce Commission. Rates are based on weight and cannot legally vary among movers. Tipping, in this line of business (unlike many others), is not requisite; it's a plus for superior service. If that's what you're given, ten dollars a man would be decent for a long-distance move.

would like to take out this secretary in my office. My associates tell me that making dates where you do business is bad business. How do you feel about it? —W. M., Ft. Madison, Wisconsin.

We feel this way: if the girl works in your department, stick strictly to business; if she's in another department, maybe, but use extreme caution if you are one who finds it difficult to disentangle himself when an affair has ended. As a rule of thumb, it is always best to avoid liaisons with anyone with whom you must be in continuous contact.

'm a girl who works in a huge downtown building, and the nature of my job requires that I ride in the elevator a great deal. Thus my question: Is it rude for a man to leave an elevator first when there are women behind him? (Many times I have to fight my way out through men who apparently feel it would be poor manners for them to exit in front of me.)— U. B., New York, New York.

It's foolish for men to block an elevator doorway while waiting for members of the fair sex to snake their way around them. In a crowded elevator, those in front, no matter what their sex, should step out first.

Although I'm no stock-market tyro, having racked up a fairly consistent record of capital gains in the last several years, there's one stock-market transaction I've never been able to understand. I know it involves both buying and selling, but tell me, please: Exactly what is "arbitrage"?—I. J., Camden, New Jersey.

You've almost go it. Arbitrage involves simultaneously purchase and sale of identical or essentially similar securities, in order to profit from price differences. Small discrepancies often occur in the price of a stock that is traded in different markets. For instance, the stock may be available on the New York exchange for $10 at the same time it's selling on the Pacific Coast exchange for $10.25. In this situation, simultaneous purchase (in New York) and sale (in San Francisco) will bring a profit of 25 cents a share (less expenses). Similarly profitable—but less apparent— price discrepancies can also occur between the conversion value of a convertible security and the security itself, or (as was the case a while back when A.T.&T. made an additional stock offering) between the rights to subscribe to a security and the security iself.

I am co-owner with another American girl of a small but lucrative café and bar in Italy. I have been having a serious affair with one of our patrons, a man who is all I've ever wanted, and who wants to marry me— but on the condition that I buy out my partner, since he thinks three's a crowd even in business. My girlfriend enjoys the life and our work here as much as I do, and I haven't had the heart to tell her of my guy's demands. What do you think I should do?—B. N., Turin, Italy.

Explain the situation to your girlfriend and give her a choice: She can either buy you out or be bought out. If you're as serious about the guy as you say you are, you should be willing to face the prospect of giving up your café, since we assume you want the man more than the business.

A close friend of mine is a writer—an absolutely brilliant person, but utterly devoid of any practical business sense. Money means little or nothing to him. Over drinks one afternoon he casually mentioned an idea—which obviously had great and immediate business potential. When I saw he was never going to do anything about it, I picked it up myself. Within a year this single idea (which I modified many times over, of course) had given birth to a profitable service business that promises to grow even more. Now I'm trying to determine my obligation to my friend, who claims he deserves nothing, since the notion grew from a conversation in which we both participated. I'm certain that he does deserve compensation—my problem is to determine what form it should take and how to get him to accept it. Can you help?—G. L., San Francisco, California.

From your letter, we can't guess how important your friend's initial idea was to the success of your business. Our impression is that his role was relatively minor—since the idea would have died a-borning if you hadn't taken it up. If this is so, and if, as you say,

*your friend is not pressing you for remuneration, then
you must let your conscience determine the reward.
A lump-sum settlement (as opposed to a percentage
or royalty agreement) would be consistent with accepted business practice, and would suit this situation.
Once you've determined the amount of the reward,
you should explain to your friend that you wish to
compensate him not just because you're a nice guy,
but because you feel genuinely indebted to him and
wish to honor same.*

For some time I have been in a quandary as to what
to do with myself. I am 26, a graduate of a prestigious
technological institute and business school. For the
past 18 months, I have been working in my profession
as an engineer. This is my first permanent, full-time
position. After college, I determined to make a go
at business by first getting my M. B. A. degree. However, during my undergraduate education I discovered
that I liked to write fiction and was encouraged in this
direction by a professor.

At present I have no personal capital and, as I
have been informed many times, "potentials are a
dime a dozen." I speak two languages and am presently studying a third, which I can by now more or
less read. I play three musical instruments (piano,
clarinet, sax) fairly well—or used to, since I haven't
practiced in years. It seems that if I continue in the
direction I am headed, I'll succeed to a degree limited
only by my perseverance. However, nothing excites
me so much that I can neither think nor talk of anything else—except, perhaps, when I write or when
I make decisions. Outside of an improbable, sudden
acquisition of sufficient no-strings finances to enable

me to pay all debts and pursue all paths of interest (including writing and such possible hobbies as sports-car racing, deep-sea fishing and polo playing), I find little in my foreseeable future that would absorb me enough to make success at it a memorable venture. What do you suggest I do?—A. V. M., Waltham, Massachusetts.

During the Renaissance, when it was possible to know the sum of human endeavor in one lifetime, certain geniuses, like Michelangelo, Da Vinci, et al., could pretend to universal knowledge. Today, even those who are geniuses, recognizing the shortness of life and the vastness of that which may be learned, generally specialize in something. In view of the fact that you're only 26 and have already dabbled in engi-neering, business and writing—occupations that gen-erally require a lifetime for mastery—and that you're not only multilingual but multimusical as well, we wonder if you can hold your own in any of these? We suggest that your inability to concentrate on a single field of endeavor betokens a crippling fear of failure. Unless you can financially afford the life of a dilettante—and apparently you cannot—you'd better eliminate the cause of your slow start (perhaps with professional help), and then move like hell to make up for it.

for better
or
for worse

for better
or for worse

"it is a woman's business
to get married as soon as possible, and a
man's to keep unmarried as long as he can,"
declared george bernard shaw, but, as g.b.s.
did finally wed, so do most men. here are some
words on when to take the step and how to
relax and enjoy the institution.

A friend of mine is about to tie the knot with a
notably knotable gal. He is a nice guy, but somewhat
strait-laced in his approach to wine, women, and song.
His other friends and I would like to toss a bachelor
party in his honor, but are undecided as to whether
the affair should be a chaste one, or whether it should
have the ribald atmosphere that is traditional at such
get-togethers. Frankly, we favor the latter.—A. J.,
Lexington, Massachusetts.

*Frankly, we don't. We have always felt that "tradi-
tional" bachelor parties, with their rib-digging humor,
single-entendres, stag flicks, and all the other indigo*

86

appurtenances, tend to verge on the poorest possible taste. Your proposed party is, or ought to be, a good-humored salute to a buddy at an unabashedly senti-mental time in his life; don't spoil it by insulting his intelligence. There are a multitude of more apropos moments for the earthier entertainments.

The girl I'm going to marry in two months is 22 and a virgin. I know she's affectionate, can even be quite passionate, but more than a few of my friends have warned me that any college graduate who's a virgin at 22 is either frigid or decidedly on the cool side. Do you think our marriage has as good a chance of surviving as it would if she were not a virgin?— G. P., Cambridge, Maryland.

Statistically, no. Kinsey's researchers found a higher percentage of divorce among married couples who had not engaged in premarital sexual intercourse than among those who had. But what is statistically true for society at large is not necessarily true for the indi-vidual. And we certainly do not agree with your friends that "any college graduate who's a virgin at 22 is either frigid or decidedly on the cool side"; virginity prior to marriage has more to do with the psyche than the sex drive. Your fiancée probably opposes pre-marital intercourse for religious-moral reasons that may in no way hinder her sexual adjustment after marriage; but it is a subject that should be thoroughly discussed and carefully considered prior to the wed-ding, for a person raised in a strong antisexual envir-onment is not always capable of setting such feelings aside with a simple "I do." Generally, it is our feeling that a successful and happy marriage is not easily achieved and every couple contemplating this impor-

*tant step should establish as many areas of compatibility
as possible. Sex is certainly not the least significant of
these.*

What are your views on a young man marrying
a woman a few years his senior?—B. P., Washington,
D.C.

*Assuming the best of circumstances—great mutual
attraction, similar interests, physical compatibility,
emotional maturity—we see nothing against it, provided the man is at least 30, and thus able to accu-
rately judge the real differences in their ages, as they
will exist for most of their lives. To a man of 21, a
girl of 26 may seem pleasingly mature, but those
same five years can become a gap of nearly a generation by the time the man reaches his late 30s or early
40s. Women age (mature, if you prefer) more rapidly
than men, even though they tend to live longer, and
this fact can cause problems for couples of even the
same age, when they marry too young: most women
in their early 20s have reached full maturity and are
the person they will be for the rest of their lives; not
so with most men. A man at 20 may be a completely
different person—different emotions, different tastes,
different interests—than the same man at 30. The
mate—of whatever age—he chooses in his early 20s
may be completely different from the girl he would
choose 10 years later. In addition, whatever differences may exist between an average man and woman
aged 20, the differences are considerably greater when
both are 40. The odds against any couple's finding
enough in common to last a lifetime are stiff enough,
under the best of circumstances, to suggest the real
wisdom of having as much going for a marriage as*

possible from the start. The ideal difference in ages, it seems to us, is about 10 years, with men marrying in their 30s and women in their 20s. More men should spend their first years out of school finding themselves, before they attempt to find a mate. Too many find a wife first and don't ever really discover who they themselves are. Or might have been.

Any opinion on wedding bands for men? I contend they have a henpecked air about them; a friend maintains that I should be proud to wear one—that is, if I'm happily married. I am, but I still think a ring on the finger is analogous to a ring through the nose.— H. K., South Bend, Indiana.

The wearing of a wedding ring is largely a matter of personal taste for the male half of a marriage, but we tend to share your prejudice and feel that a gold band on the third finger, left hand of a man suggests less a happy marriage than a henpecked hubby, who wears it to keep out of trouble at, and away from, home; or else a guy so egocentric that he considers himself irresistible to the opposite sex and thinks he needs the wedding band to fend off other hopeful females.

I've been divorced for some years, and in recent months have been dating a delightful young woman whom I met while skiing last winter. She and I have become quite close, and therein lies the problem. For some reason in our initial dates I never got around to telling her I'd been married previously, and now I gather from the tone of some of our conversations

89

that she has a vague objection to divorce as an institution. (She's never said as much, but has strongly implied it on several occasions.) We're getting more and more serious, and I've been toying with the idea of asking her to marry me. At this late date, should I risk ending our relationship by revealing my earlier marriage?—W. D., St. Louis, Missouri.

Tell her, by all means—you should have done so long ago. Only by getting the matter out in the open will you discover her real feelings—of which you should certainly be apprised before you even consider marriage. If her objections still persist after you've thoroughly discussed your divorce with her, you should forget those marriage thoughts, because such a psychological (or religious) barrier would make any permanent union perilous.

■'m engaged to a girl who's good-looking, intelligent and quite passionate. We have been intimate for more than a year, and we find ourselves physically compatible. The problem is that we often disagree—sometimes quite violently—over relatively small matters. Our latest set-to-, for instance, was provoked by the question of whether I should order theater tickets for balcony or orchestra. The result was that we stayed at my pad and seethed for most of the evening, then finally patched things up. A friend of mine, whose opinion I respect, has questioned the wisdom of our projected marriage. Do you think we can make a go of it?—C. M., Chicago, Illinois.

Not as things are now. The fact that you are physically compatible is no assurance that your marriage will succeed, though it is an important leg up. The fact that you have frequent heated arguments over

*subjects as trivial as where to sit in the theater estab-
lishes these disagreements as a cover-up for deeper
differences and resentments. We advise you to postpone your wedding until you find out what these might
be—either talk it out between yourselves or get professional help in untangling your conflicting psyches.*

A close friend of mine is getting married in Canada
and has asked me to be best man. This creates a
problem because I am low on funds at present and
unable to afford the trip. The groom has offered to
pay my fare, reasoning that he should compensate me
for my loss of working time. But since he is just
starting out, would it be rude of me to accept his
generosity?—W. D., Sparks, Nevada.

*Not at all. Your friend obviously wants you to be
his best man despite the additional expense. Saving
him from altar-falter is far more important than saving a few dollars. Go to the wedding and have a good
time.*

Since I have exhausted my own ideas, I would
like a few from you. My problem is with the girl to
whom I am all but engaged. We have a wonderful
and very satisfying relationship in every respect but
one—we disagree markedly over the status of her
education. She has had but one year of college (which
she enjoyed) and is now working as a secretary.
I have already earned one postgraduate degree and
am well on my way to the second, so there is a vast
educational gap between us.

This problem has bothered me from the beginning

of the relationship and I have tried many different approaches to induce her to return to school, but all have had little or no success. She has refused to think about more formal education, even after I asked her a dozen or so questions on current events ranging from "Who is the Chief Justice of the Supreme Court?" to "Who is Charles de Gaulle?" and she scored a flat zero! This girl is genuinely in love with me and wants to get married soon; but no matter how I try, subtly, pleadingly or forcefully, I can get nowhere on this one subject. How do I get this girl to develop her intellect to a level that matches her physical attributes and wonderful personality? —D. S., Oakland, California.

We know some kids in elementary school who would have scored well on your test; we also know some university grads who might have flunked it. The mere possession of a degree, unfortunately, neither assures a complete education or heightens an individual's awareness of what's going on in the world. Since you seek intellectual companionship in your marriage, this girl is probably the wrong one for you.

Please forgive what I fear may be a dreadful intrusion into the private masculinity of your magazine. But I have a problem that (alas) no woman's magazine would dare answer. My problem is simply that I was foolish enough never to have been anyone's playmate until my husband and I were married, and now I feel the lack of experience is woefully apparent. Could you please help me?—L. R., Albuquerque, New Mexico.

Hell no—your husband might walk in! But he can —and should—help you by (1) being patient, and (2)

*buying any one of several good books on the subject
of sexual technique. (Among them: "The Marriage
Art" by Dr. John E. Eichenlaub; "The Art of Love"
by Dr. W. F. Robie; "The Art and Science of Love"
by Dr. Albert Ellis; "Sex: Methods and Manners" by
Louis Berg and Robert Street; and Havelock Ellis'
classic, "The Dance of Life.")*

How can I persuade a wealthy girl that I want to
marry her for love, and not for her money alone?—
F. S., Palm Beach, Florida.

*Are you sure you're leveling with yourself? That
word "alone" suggests mixed motives. Regardless of
your motives, tell her you plan to get married and if
she won't have you, you'll look elsewhere. There's an
off-chance this gambit won't work. If it doesn't, you
may find another rich girl who'll be your wife. If this
thought is comforting, the girl is right.*

After a normal courtship and engagement, my
fiancée suddenly insisted that before the wedding I
must get sterilized. I readily agreed and made arrangements to have a vasectomy. More recently, however,
I have wondered about the motivation behind her
ultimatum. Should I go ahead with the operation or
send my fiancée to a psychiatrist?—J. J., Detroit,
Michigan.

*Even if you are willing to enter into a marriage
with no intention of having children, with today's
birth-control techniques, we think it would be foolish
for you to go ahead with such an operation, or with
the marriage either, for that matter. You have good*

93

reason to wonder about the motivation behind your fiancée's sudden ultimatum: It sounds like a deep-seated, irrational fear of pregnancy; and there may be a little subconscious castration hostility hidden away there, too. In either case, your chances of establishing a successful marriage with this girl are slight. Yes, psychiatric consultation certainly seems called for here; and it might be a good idea to set aside a couple of sessions for yourself, too—to probe your ready agreement to this symbolic castration in the first place.

Most of your comments are understandably directed to the cause of preserving bachelors from gaucherie and cloying alliances, but the question of standards affecting the young married set seems also to need a definitive—or at least an honest—answer. My bride and I, now in our early 30s, have successfully made our way through the threadbare postcollege years, and with the kids in school and a comfortable income assured, are beginning to enjoy some leisure and expand our horizons once again. Herein lies the problem: one of the girls in our crowd is a delightful creature with whom I could enjoy a relationship more personal than that of a bridge partner, and the feeling is clearly reciprocated. Similarly, her husband and my wife are developing an equally sympathetic rapport. Lately the four of us have been talking about a weekend boating trip together, and the tacit understanding seems to be that the port and starboard watches will be subject to an exchange of personnel for the voyage, isolated from the prying eyes of those with a proclivity to gossip. The stumbling block, of course, is the insistence by so-called "experts" on marital relations that this sort of hanky-panky will rot the moral fiber, cause ulcers, falling hair, and presumably, the gout. The illogic of this position is that the alternative can only be secret, hasty extramarital flings, with all the guilt that such dishonesty produces. We are sophisticated happily married adults seeking an intelligent answer to what must be a widespread problem. Don't you think this is one area where there is room for a fresh reappraisal of standards? Your magazine seems to be the only source of healthy thinking on the development of social and sexual mores under today's conditions.—S. M., Galveston, Texas.

We seriously doubt that the arrangement you suggest will produce a more satisfying, healthy and happy marriage. Wife swapping is not really an "alternative" to the dishonestly of an illicit affair—both are symptomatic of an inadequacy in the marriage or in one of the marriage partners. This sort of mixed doubles may not cause ulcers, falling hair or the gout, but only the most unemotional and sophisticated of couples could sail through such rough, uncharted waters without any effect on their relationship. We suggest that you stow the plans for a switcheroo and concentrate on expanding your horizons—both in and out of bed—together, rather than with some outside party or pair.

The banns have been published and the banalities preached but I'm still at a loss on one problem: how intimate a gift may I bestow on a girl to whom I'm engaged but am not yet entwined?—J. G., Miami Beach, Florida.

A man's gifts to his betrothed should reflect his tastes, his tact and his tactics. If you believe in tradition, festoon her with fancies that may be seen from the outside (scarves, gloves, jewelry), and don't skin-

dive for flimsies worn under the surface. Convention flouters who see no point in refraining from the familiar may, on the other hand, win approbation by shopping in the undergarment district. If the girl has a sense of humor, you might also present her a fancily wrapped package with a note reading "To be worn on our wedding night"—first insuring, of course, that the package is pristinely empty.

You have on several different occasions stated your objections to men marrying young, but I gather you do not feel the same way about women. I'm 19, in love with a man (divorced, no children) in his 30s. I am confident that our marriage (set for early spring) will be a success, but in the light of your earlier assertions, I'm curious to learn your views toward this impending union.—B. M., Charlottesville, Virginia.

Census Bureau figures show that more than 60 percent of all American girls marry before age 22, which is many more girls than we'd care to argue with. Though your chances of making a lasting marriage might increase if you wait a few years before taking the plunge, it's the age of the male that seems to be the single most important statistical factor in determining whether a marriage will flower or flop. Thus, the marriage of a girl 19 to a man in his 30s probably has a greater chance of success than the marriage of the same girl to a man in his early 20s. And good luck.

Last year I was married for two weeks to a college girl in North Carolina. Our breakup occurred because she refused to move to the town where I work. Now I want to marry a French girl I met in Montreal, but I'm worried about telling her of my first marriage. Since it was such a short affair, should I just forget that it ever happened?—E. S., Long Branch, New Jersey.

Just why you're afraid to tell your new fiancée about that first marriage isn't clear. But we'll assume that it's because she might realize you're not ready for a second one. And for our money, you're not. Any guy who could get married without first discussing such obvious issues as residence, should have stood in the stag line. Now you seem prepared to make a no-questions-answered leap again. We suggest you hold off until you can tell the girl all the facts about yourself—including your first mistake. By the way, you are divorced, aren't you?

Shel and I were married four years ago at the respective ages of 27 and 23. He had been in the Navy, worked two years, and was then a junior in medical school. My salary was our sole source of income for three years, and a necessary supplement during internship. He's now a resident, and is perfectly willing for me to give up my job, but he's far from willing to start a family. I think I could hound him into granting permission, but I don't know whether I should.

I love Shel very much, and we get along famously. We both fly his airplane, and have often decided on Friday afternoons to go to the Caribbean, New York, etc., without worrying about a baby sitter. Of course, I've enjoyed all this, too, but I *want* a baby. Shel thinks this would be an "unnecessary and expensive millstone." What do you think would happen if I just

97

"forgot" a few pink pills and sprang a baby on him? Is it possible that he'd hate it and I'd have a little phychotic on my hands? Would this be better or worse than making him angry and depressed with constant begging? Help!—Mrs. P. Z., Atlanta, Georgia.

While we sympathize with your desire to be a mother, we can also understand your husband's wish not to be tied down, especially since he's recently completed the rigorous medical school grind. It would be unthinkable for you to have a baby without his consent. Not only might this action be harmful to the child, but its dishonesty would assuredly implant a seed of malignancy into what seems to be a healthy marriage. Ordinarily, we'd advise talking the problem out, but you've obviously had plenty of conversations on this subject. Why don't you drop it and wait a couple of years? (You'll still be under 30.) Let Shel enjoy his freedom for a while, and try to enjoy it with him. Relieved of your constant pressure, and in a more fluid financial position, he may then change his mind.

have a problem that I'm sure isn't unusual, but it's perplexing. In about a month I'm going to be the best man at a wedding. What exactly are my responsibilities? While I'm glad to help my friend get married, I'm wondering if being best man will take all the fun out of it.—A. D., Charlottesville, Virginia.

On the contrary, you've got the best seat in the house. You'll attend the bachelor party beforehand and the reception afterward; you'll get to be first with the champagne, and to enjoy such nuptial perquisites as kissing the bride—all without having to marry anybody. You will have many duties, however, and the success of the wedding may depend on how efficiently you dispatch them. First of all, you'll see that the ushers are suitably and uniformly dressed for the occasion (in accordance with the wishes of the bride's family) and are clearly instructed and rehearsed on their churchly functions. You'll make the arrangements for the bachelor dinner, too, if there is one. You will also be the one who helps the groom dress for the ceremony and reminds him to tuck the marriage license into a convenient pocket. Above all, you must get him to the church on time—at least half an hour before the ceremony—and while you're offering him last-minute moral support in the vestry, double-check your own pockets to make sure you've got the ring and the fee for the ceremony (in a plain envelope which you should slip discreetly to the officiating clergyman immediately after the vows). At the reception, though it isn't de rigueur, you'll want to help keep the champagne flowing and the reception line moving smoothly past the newlyweds. You'll be expected to arrange for such details of departure as plane tickets, car keys, and the like. And you'll be the man who stashes the bride's and groom's luggage safely in their getaway car, and takes care of the groom's post-nuptial quick change into street clothes. If you're a first-drawer best man, you'll also see to it that there are a chilled bottle of bubbly and two glasses in the car—to which you will later clear a path for the bride and groom. And one last duty: Keep your mouth shut about where they're going to spend the night.

Shortly after I began my tour of duty in West Germany, I met a lovely German girl with whom I subsequently fell in love and proposed marriage. My family is very open-minded about my marrying a foreign national, but I am encountering a great deal of resistance from my ex-fiancée back home. She has repeatedly sent letters to my intended's family enumerating the possible hazards involved in such a marriage and, although I don't particularly care for this invasion of my privacy, I have held off putting a stop to it for one very good reason. You see, my military career is just about at an end, and I have been promised a job paying $14,000 per year by my ex-fiancée's father, providing I give up my German girl and marry his daughter. It's not that I place money above romance, but $14,000 a year shouldn't be taken lightly, and I just can't seem to solve this "mating dilemma." Any suggestions?—E. W., Wiesbaden, West Germany.

First, we suggest you stop kidding yourself about being a latent romanticist. The fact that you describe this situation in such cold, cash-on-the-line terms leaves little doubt that you won't allow a five-figure annuity to slip through your fingers. Ordinarily we'd advise going where your heart leads—most people who place a price tag on their emotions find it more expensive in the end than they bargained for—but in your case, it's obvious that you don't consider your present fiancée a good long-term investment. You could patch things up with your ex, but we doubt that a lifetime contract based on the sort of setup you describe would bring much happiness to anyone involved. We suggest you solve your mating dilemma by breaking cleanly with both girls—and then waiting until you grow up. You're obviously not ready for marriage.

I'm engaged to marry a girl who is all I want in a wife. Her parents, while not wealthy, are well off.

When each of her three older sisters married, her father, who is a warm and generous man, gave the newlyweds a fat cash gift, followed up periodically with additional presents. I assume he plans the same for us, and, quite frankly, I would rather not accept the money. Not that it wouldn't come in handy: It's just that in the long run I'd rather have self-respect than dough. What are your feelings?—J. G., New York, New York.

A cash gift, if it's forthcoming, will be simply a wedding present. We have nothing against wedding gifts, and in this instance feel that you would be insulting your future father-in-law by refusing what he offered. Of course, after you're married, you would be justified in refusing additional largess, if that is your preference, but we fail to see how your self-respect is jeopardized if there are no strings attached to the moola.

The girl I'm engaged to is a good deal brighter than I am, and I wonder if our marriage will fade in the stretch because of this marked difference. Please understand: I'm no dummy, having successfully negotiated college and landed a rewarding technical job. It's just that my fiancée bats in another league—she graduated Phi Beta from a top women's college and plans to go on for a master's and a Ph.D. We have a successful relationship and, despite our differences, find a lot to talk about. However, I'm a little skeptical about the long run.—B. B., Woburn, Massachusetts.

Since you have a successful relationship and do find a lot to talk about, the vast differences you cite may be just so much academic applesauce. You obviously have a lot in common, or you never would

*have become engaged; and, we assume, your attrac-
tion to each other is more than just physical (or isn't
it?). Possibly you're underestimating your own abilities
and overestimating your girl's. If you do have grave
doubts even after prolonged soul-searching on the
durability of your relationship, we would advise you
to break your engagement and seek a less intellectually well-endowed chick with whom you will feel
more at ease in the traditional male role.*

I am 34 years old and divorced. I had been dating
an 18-year-old girl for several months and we had
fallen in love, but her father disapproved and shipped
her out of town to forget me. This only served to
reinforce our feelings and now we are determined to
get married. If we do, can her father do anything to
legally separate us?—M. J., Inglewood, California.

*You'll have to ask an attorney what her dad can
legally do to keep you and your girl apart, but at the
moment it sounds as if he's doing all he can to push
you two together. If you wed his darling daughter
simply to defy him—which you say you're "determined"
to do—all three of you could wind up losers.*

I've been engaged to a girl for a year and a half and
contemplate marriage in the very near future. There's
one dark cloud on what looks like a very bright hori-
zon; she has been under psychoanalysis for the last
three years. Her family, who can afford it, spends
seventy-five dollars a week on couch fees. I have a
pretty fair job but not good enough yet to handle the
tab on her thrice-a-week sessions. Shall we postpone

the wedding until she's out of analysis (no way of telling when that might be), take the plunge and try to handle the doctor bills as best we can, or accept her parents' offer to continue paying for the therapy until she's out of it? The latter really rubs me the wrong way, but I love the girl and want to do whatever's best for her. What do you think?—B. G., Tucson, Arizona.

We would advise holding the wedding in abeyance until she finishes her analysis, and not for monetary reasons. Marriage is a giant, emotion-jarring step, and might conceivably complicate the situation and aggravate your girl's problems. There are enough adjustments to make under normal conditions without additional psychological stumbling blocks thrown in. It might help clear the air to discuss the impending nuptials with her analyst, if he's willing, and find out from him whether marriage would be a wise move.

Although my fiancée and I agree that we would like to raise a family, we cannot agree on what religion our children should follow. I am Catholic and she is Lutheran, but we both feel that a common religion should be adopted in order to facilitate our future children's welfare. Our parents also insist that we decide on one faith between us, but, to tell the truth, neither of us is particularly fond of the other's faith. I respect my fiancée's right to her religious beliefs, and she respects mine; but when it comes to choosing a mutual religious denomination, each prefers his own. Can this dilemma be resolved, or does it look fairly hopeless to you, too?—M. R., New York, New York.

If you're not using your religious differences to hide the fact that you actually don't want to marry the girl (a possibility suggested by your asking us to agree that the situation is hopeless), there are several approaches open to you. Each of you could study the other's faith, to develop respect for it, and you could then mutually decide later in which one you wish to raise your future offspring. Or you could bring up the children in a religion that tries to reconcile doctrinal differences—for example, the Unitarian-Universalist Church, or the Ethical Culture movement. Or, if you don't wish to make even these compromises, there is in your own city the Community Church, 40 East 35th Street, which accepts persons of all persuasions, while respecting their religious identities. You could enroll your children there as Lutheran-Catholics, which is exactly what they would be.

I am a sailor, single, and stationed in Morocco. I have been here for ten months and have become extremely fond of a Moroccan girl. My problem: She is a lady of the night. Normally this would preclude any thought of marriage, but in Moroccan society it is acceptable for a girl of little means to engage in prostitution to earn money for her dowry. Since this custom is not proscribed in Moslem society, is it fair to judge her in terms of Western morality? Ignoring her profession, she is an exceedingly attractive and marriageable young woman. Neither she nor I have any particular religious beliefs, so no problems are posed here. Under no circumstances would I relate to my family this girl's personal history. Considering the factors involved, what do you think of our chances? —J. E. F., Fleet Post Office, New York.

So-so. Any marriage of individuals of drastically different backgrounds invites more than its quota of problems—which is usually large enough without any outside help. Your girl's profession is only one of the obstacles you face. There's also conflicting nationality, culture and language. We don't mean to suggest that these barriers can't be overcome, or that you can't achieve a successful union. You can, but only if you really know what you're getting into. The fact that the girl is a prostitute is perhaps the least of your worries. Prostitutes work for money, rarely for fun, and once the economic need is relieved, they can be just as chaste as the proverbial girl next door. You've got to decide whether you can face the variety of prejudices you'll encounter, bearing in mind that even if you dissemble about her past, some relic of it may return to embarrass you. But if, between the two of you, you can defeat these problems, the rapport you develop in so doing may help you build a better marriage than most.

I was a virgin at marriage and my wife was not. Since my discovery of her several former relationships, I have endured periodic fits of depression. I don't consider my wife as chattel, and we have a sound intellectual and physical relationship. But still, I worry. Can you help?—J. B., Chicago, Illinois.

We can only help by reaffirming our belief that when you scratch a jealous lover you uncover an angry proprietor. You obviously do consider your wife as chattel; if you didn't, you'd have no worries. The desire to possess your wife's past (which had nothing to do with you and is no business of yours now) is possessiveness to the nth degree. Having married a virgin, your wife has more cause for worry than you do, and if she's satisfied, you certainly should be.

■ 'm a sales engineer for an electronics firm and my job keeps me on the road for at least six months of the year. While I'm here in L. A., I see one girl steadily, but naturally enough, I have casual girl-friends in many of the other cities on my itinerary. Mostly at her instigation, I've been toying with the idea of marrying my Los Angeles girl, who understands that our marriage would necessarily be an on-and-off proposition, with me out of the house at least half the time. She says she'd be content with such an arrangement, and realizes that to ask me to be faithful to her for my six months away from home would be asking too much. She's ready to name the date, but I *still* have my reservations. Do you feel I should go ahead with this marriage?—P. T., Los Angeles, California.

No, we don't. We think your reservations are well founded. Until you're interested enough in a relationship to want it on more than a part-time basis, you'll be wise to avoid matrimony altogether. The odds against establishing a successful marriage on such a casual and uncommitted basis are astronomical.

▲ girl I've been dating steadily is—by all indications —an alcoholic. Though when she's with me I can usually keep her off the bottle, she frankly admits that one or two nights a week she'll drink herself senseless in the privacy of her own apartment. When she's sober, she's as fine a girl as I've ever known; I've even been thinking of asking her to marry me, on the assumption that once I have her under my wing I'll be able to get her to kick her drinking habit. What are your thoughts?—G. K., Waco, Texas.

We think you're mistaken in thinking that marriage can cure alcoholism. Uncontrollable drinking is not only a sickness itself, it can also be a symptom of a more serious psychological illness which should be treated professionally. You should guide this girl into the hands of Alcoholics Anonymous, or to a psychiatrist, or both, and put off any thoughts of marriage until you're satisfied that she's off the sauce, or that she has her drinking under control.

I am a very technically inclined person and rather than waste time and money at night clubs and dances, I would like to use science to find the sort of mate I am looking for. I have heard of computers being used to make matches on the basis of similar interests. My question is this: Where are these machines located and how does one get in touch with the people operating them?—R. M., Bridgeport, Connecticut.

The organization you seek is Scientific Marriage Institute, located at 185 East 73rd Street, New York, New York 10021. But be careful—the machine might want to keep you for itself.

I am 28, married, and a successful engineer. However, I find that the social life that my wife and I are active in is threatening our happy marriage. Somehow, after Saturday evening cut, our group (which consists of couples our age, who have been married for much longer than we have) always ends at my home—which is the most attractive—for that last drink. That last drink, however usually turns out to be more of the same, with dancing and conversation. A distinct temptation at these late, intimate, boozy parties is to make advances toward someone else's mate. I would

like to stop these parties and cultivate other friendships, but I'm afraid that even new friends might lead
to the same story.—B. F., Hartford, Connecticut.

*If that old gang is breaking up those wedding bells
of yours, the solution is to find a new, less ram-
bunctious gang. However, your feeling that even new
friends would "lead to the same story" suggests that
perhaps you and your wife unconsciously want it that
way. Talk it over seriously and honestly with her
(that's one of the things wives are for)—and may we
suggest you have your talk alone, at home, next
Saturday night.*

The guy I'm engaged to refuses to have sexual relations with me. Though I've tried womanly wiles, he
always retreats, with the explanation that he's "saving"
me for our marriage. As a consequence, I am cha-
grined to admit that I've been seeing another man on
the sly. I don't like sneaky sex, and I don't like carrying on behind my fiancé's back. However, I am a
healthy woman, with a healthy woman's desires. Can
you help me out of this situation?—P. M., New
Orleans, Louisiana.

*If you've been unable to melt your fiancé with the
heat of your premarital charms, it will probably take
more than a trip down the aisle to do the trick. Though
he may believe he's "saving" you for marriage, there's
a good chance his moral posture covers a long-estab-
lished antagonism to sex, at least with the girl he
intends to marry, because he subconsciously considers
the sexual act degrading for women. In addition, the
two of you obviously have diametrically opposed views
of sexual morality, which could trigger the most violent kind of reaction should he ever learn that an-*

other has been withdrawing what he's been "saving."
We think a marriage under such circumstances would
be foolhardy and courting almost certain disaster; you
would be wise to break off the engagement at once.

Last year one of our foursome got married and the
rest of our group gave a party for him and his bride
that will never be forgotten. As a matter of fact, it
was written up in *The Kansas City Star*. Unfortunately,
another of our group is getting married this year and
three of us are faced with outdoing or at least equal-
ing our last fete. As matters stand now, we are trans-
porting our 35 guests from a predetermined meeting
place to the party spot (a farm) by helicopter. We
have engaged two groups (a Western combo and a
rolled-up-sleeves-type piano player) to provide continuous entertainment, but, since this is an outdoor
party, we are stumped for a really wide-open-spaces
type menu. One of our ideas is to barbecue half a
buffalo on a spit, but that seems too ordinary. We're
in desperate need of a way-out idea for food, and
would appreciate your help.—R. L., Kansas City,
Missouri.

The only dish we could come up with that's farther
out than barbecued buffalo is the following recipe
(for which we're indebted to Alexandre Dumas) for
sautéed kangaroo filet. (To serve 35, multiply all quan-
tities by 17½.)

"Take 2 fillets, trim, season, and arrange in a pot
with melted butter. In another pot, prepare a broth
from the bones and scraps of meat from the animal,
strain, remove the fat. Pour into a pot with 4 table-
spoonfuls of vinegar, add a bouquet garni, reduce to
a light sauce, add 2 tablespoonfuls of currant jelly and

a piece of lemon zest. Ten minutes later, add a hand-
ful of raisins soaked in warm water. Let the whole
simmer about one hour. Poach the fillets, drain, set
them on a platter and pour the sauce over them."

You have answered questions about marriage problems of women in your column before, so here I go.
What do I do about a girl who's crying on my husband's shoulder about her love affairs with other married men? He talks so much about her that I get
a sick feeling when he mentions her name. He insists
that she's "just a kid" (18) and that he wouldn't date
her even if he were single, but I notice he's beginning
to lose interest in our two children. And recently he
said to me, "You're so young and beautiful and your
world has been in this apartment for four years now;
you've got to get out more with me." Well, I find
nothing boring about my housewife's job, so it seems
to me he's just trying to provide me with a social life
so he can let me down easy before he asks for his
freedom. I'm not going to fall to pieces if you tell me
he loves her and that divorce is the answer. Just let
me know.—B. L., Hudson, Massachusetts.

Sweetheart, relax. Rather than trying to let you
down gently, he is trying to tell you—although perhaps
unconsciously—that you have let him down. You've
been so busy being unbored with your "housewife's
job" that you've deprived him of the feeling of being
needed. Why not "fall to pieces" when you're fright-
ened? After all, there wouldn't be any room on his
shoulder for another girl's tears if yours were there.
Stop being so self-contained, go out with him when
he wants you to, and let him into your private universe
before it's too late. Our hunch is that you really do

*need him, but you haven't let him—or yourself—
know it.*

■ have just about lost my mind thinking about my
ex-girlfriend. We dated steadily for over two years
and she told me she had no interest in any other men
and loved me very much. Then, last month, she shot
me down so abruptly that I still don't quite know what
happened. Her reasons were that we were becoming
too serious (I never proposed marriage) and she
didn't want the responsibility of being romantically
involved How do I get her back?—S. B., Gettysburg,
Pennsylvania.

*You have been kissed off—firmly and forever. There
can be a million reasons why, but we suspect that
what she told you is the truth. It is no reflection on
you. By freeing you from an unrequited relationship,
the young lady has actually done you a favor.*

■ am having letter trouble. For a year or so I was
involved with a girl in a long and mutually gratifying
affair, which was abetted by a good deal of correspondence. I admit that I got a bit impetuous in
some of my letters to her and I stated my affection
in extremely warm tones. A couple of months ago
the romance went on the rocks—our break was a bit
messy, and a lot of angry words were spoken. I have
since started dating another girl and things have been
going fine. But here's the rub—the two chicks know
each other, and the ex-girlfriend, still claiming I gave
her a raw deal, has threatened to turn over my love
letters to girl number two. Her idea, obviously, is not

only to embarrass me, but to show me up as some kind of unscrupulous hypocrite who hands out the same line to everyone who comes along. I'd like to know if she can get away with this. Technically speaking, aren't those letters mine? After all, I wrote them. I want to get them back.—S. K., Baltimore, Maryland.

Unfortunately, since a postmarked letter becomes the legal property of the recipient and not the sender, your jilted Jezebel has every right to share your scarlet letters with whomever she wishes. Your only recourse is to explain to your current miss that these missives are overstatements of an honest emotion which you no longer feel. Perhaps you'll be able to persuade her that reading them would constitute a breach of faith, and a useless raking over of coals that have long since gone cold. In the future, we suggest you curb your enthusiasm when penning amorous notes. As William Makepeace Thackeray once astutely observed, "The best way is to make your letters safe. I never wrote a letter in all my life that would commit me and, sir, I have had some experience of women." Unlettered love, in other words, usually spells wisdom.

on
the
town . . .

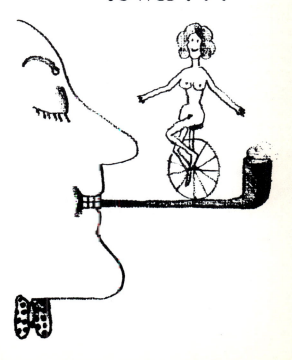

on the town...

the modern man is well in tune
with the excitement of urban living.
the city's lights are to him a brilliant
backdrop for wining, dining and dancing.
this section, then, is for those
who would be wise to the ways
of the metropolis.

Being a young, single male, gainfully employed, with no physical deformities, I am what is known in social circles as a highly eligible bachelor. In this regard, I am invited to an endless procession of dinner parties, cocktail parties, after-theater parties, and purposeless parties—almost all of which are thrown by hostesses, gracious and otherwise. Up till now, I've considered it sufficient acknowledgment of my hostess' labors to thank her profusely for the grand time and/or the wonderful dinner as I was departing. I've now been told by people whose judgment I usually respect, that I've been a boorish guest for not offering a more formal acknowledgment of my having been entertained—by either a follow-up phone

114

call, a letter or flowers. I can't believe that, in this day and age, such Victorian protocol still exists. Does it?—F. S., Philadelphia, Pennsylvania.

It does. The time and effort involved if you phone, or write a note, is minimal, as is the expense if you send flowers. Give it a try; you'll see that it won't hurt a bit.

At a wild party last weekend, my girl-friend—who is not much of a drinker—got absolutely soused, stripped down to panties and bra, and did an imitation of Doris Day—before passing out. I must admit I was a little high myself, otherwise I probably could have prevented the display. Though everyone thought it was a lark at the time, my girl is now so embarrassed that she refuses to go anyplace where she might encounter witnesses to her performance. Since this was a big party and our friends get around a lot, her reluctance to be seen has seriously cramped our social life. I think she's being silly, don't you?—C. G., Chicago, Illinois.

Yes—although we find her embarrassment over imitating Doris Day perfectly understandable. As for the rest of her conduct, try pointing out that since your friends didn't disapprove of her lark while it was in flight, they probably don't object to it in retrospect either. If this doesn't solve the problem, we suspect that a little time will.

I own an XK-E, which presents me with an interesting problem: It's so low that the skirts of my dates tend to ride up when they're getting out of the car.

As I hold the door, should I discreetly avert my eyes, or turn my back altogether? Or should I suggest that the demoiselles making their entrances and exits unassisted?—K. F., Washington, D. C.

Keep your eyes on your work, which in this case, is assisting your dates from your car. Girls have a surprisingly acute awareness of when and what they're showing, and the auto exit is a traditionally acceptable scene for a bit of healthy exhibitionism. Don't let your gentlemanly instinct spoil what amounts to good clean fun; if you look away too often, your girls might get the idea you don't like the view.

I'm faced with a touchy problem. I have been invited to a dinner party next month, and the girl I plan to take is a Negro (I'm white). Would I insult either hostess or date by calling the hostess in advance to inform her of my intention?—J. P., New York, New York.

Yes, you would. This sort of pussyfooting is tantamount to giving aid and comfort to the enemy. Certainly your girl has encountered prejudice before, and most likely she will again. With you at her side, it's doubtful that she'll be seriously distressed by any possible turn of events during the course of the evening. And probably, in a sophisticated, urban setting, the evening will pass pleasantly and without incident.

The other day, while we were out walking, my girl introduced me to a female friend of hers. When the friend held out her hand, I took it without removing my glove. Afterward, my girl raised holy hell and said if I had any "couth" at all I would know enough not to hand a woman leather instead of skin when introductions were being made. I say this bit went out with Sir Gawain. Who's right?—H. L., Seattle, Washington.

You are. In days of yore, failure to remove one's glove when greeting a woman was always deemed rude; today, it's perfectly OK to handle her with kid gloves when their removal would be awkward or time-consuming.

The other night I wined and dined a lovely young thing at one of our city's best restaurants. The tab was around $35—money well spent, as it turned out. But I happened to notice that the bill contained an addition error—amounting to a one-dollar overcharge. Rather than make a scene over such a small amount, I just paid it. In retrospect, however, I feel I should have made a fuss. What's your opinion?—J. W., Baltimore, Maryland.

No reason to make a "fuss," as you put it. You should have asked that your bill be added up again; a polite request would certainly have done the trick.

I would like your opinion on a unique experience. Recently, I had a blind date with a divorcée, arranged through a mutual friend. As I was taking her home—after an evening of wining, dining and dancing—she informed me that I would have to pay her baby sitter. I felt justified in *not* paying the sitter, but she didn't see it my way. She said that if I was to have the pleasure of her company, I should be prepared to cover all

117

expenses. I finally agreed to pay half the sitter's fee, but I was damned displeased. Do you think that my companion's demand was proper?—H. F., Dallas, Texas.

No, her demand wasn't proper, but neither was your haggling with her over the few dollars it must have cost to pay the sitter. What you should have done was tell your date before the evening started that you were going to take care of the sitting fee. The lady's officious attitude might have given you good cause to scratch her off your date list, but that in no way should have precluded your acting like a gentleman and not like a penny-pinching clod.

The other night my girl and I dated with another couple, dining at one of the best restaurants in town. She and I are both light eaters and ordered accordingly, but the other couple began putting food away like it was going out of style. The bill came to $40, of which our half was no more than $12. When this chap slipped me $20 and said, "Here's my half," I hit the ceiling. I demanded then and there that he cough up enough dough to cover that part of the bill he and his cohort had run up. We parted with no love lost, and my girl subsequently chided me for not having gone along with the 50–50 split. Should I have?— O. B., New Orleans, Louisiana.

The whole idea of haggling over a check at the dinner table is very unappetizing. You could have done one of two things, either of which is infinitely better than ticking off who had what drinks and what desserts: You could have paid the whole tab and told your friend that the next dinner would be on him, or you could have told him you'd settle up later, out

*of earshot of your dates, and taken whatever he
offered as his end of the bill. If you thought he was
taking advantage of you, you should have chalked it
up to experience.*

At most of the best restaurants in the Midwest, the
salad is served *before* the entree. In New York, the
salad is served *after* the entree. I have learned this,
to my considerable embarrassment, by asking for salad
after finishing my appetizer, only to have New York
waiters look at me as if I were a boob. What's the
story?—L. M., Chicago, Illinois.

*Confusion rises from the fact that conflicting cus-
toms govern the serving of salad. The so-called Russian
Service—originated back in the days of the czars—
required the serving of each course separately, and
removal of the soiled plates before the next course
was served The English Service was strictly groaning
board: all the food was put on the table at the same
time, with the diners helping in carving, serving and
passing. Haute Cuisine restaurants usually adhere to
the Russian Service; salad may be served before the
entree providing it is the kind of salad that is suitable
as an hors d'oeuvre, otherwise it is served after the entree. It is the use of dressed cold vegetables (raw
or cooked) as hors d'oeuvres that has led to the service
of salad before the entree in some more primitive parts
of the U.S., but to precede this salad with the usual
appetizers doesn't conform with good sense—or good
custom in the restaurants that pay homage to France
by following the Haute Cuisine order of service. So,
wherever you are, if you start a meal with an appetizer, ask for—or gracefully accept—salad after your
entree. Only a boob would do otherwise.*

Recently a casual girlfriend and I double-dated with another couple I know only vaguely, using his car. When we reached the club where we were to dine, my date decided to leave her coat in the car, which we didn't bother to lock. When we returned, the coat (brand new) had been stolen. It turned out to be a $600 item, uninsured, and my date said she thought we guys were pikers since we didn't offer to help pay for it. Do you think we were right?—W. A., Gulfport, Mississippi.

Yes. Though it's unfortunate you didn't lock the car, even that would not have guaranteed the coat's safety. Possession of a valuable article carries responsibilities in which your date was negligent. She was remiss in not having the coat insured; and certainly she could have taken it with her and checked it at your club. The fault was hers, not yours, and the fact that it was his car does not affect the matter.

Some close friends of mine are members of a private club that I'd very much like to join. Would it be proper for me simply to ask them to try to get me in?
—K. A., Lake Forest, Illinois.

No. What makes a private club private is its members' right of selection. The best you can do is hint at your interest—obliquely and discreetly—and wait for your friends to take the initiative. If they don't—forget it.

I have an invitation to a very formal affair, at which I want to be impeccably turned out. I believe that I have all the necessary gear, save for one item: shoes.

A friend tells me that opera pumps are essential when a man wears a tuxedo. Trouble is, I object to the bows that one finds on opera pumps—they strike me as swish rather than swank. Would I be committing a serious *faux pas* if I wore plain black shoes?—L. C., St. Louis, Missouri.

No. While opera pumps are de rigueur *with tails, they are optional with a tuxedo. Either a plain formal dress shoe or a plain black shoe is an acceptable compromise.*

Would you name some nonalcoholic drinks that a guy on the wagon can ask for without attracting attention or seeming to be a prig? I'm staying dry for a month (not a bet—doc's orders), but I do want to continue to be my convivial, gregarious self—as much as I can under these arid circumstances.—A. N., Bowling Green, Ohio.

At bars, you can ask for a Horse's Neck (rind of lemon curled over the lip of a highball glass filled with ice and ginger ale); a Bloody Awful (a Bloody Mary sans the vodka); a Nellie Collins (Tom Collins without gin); a glass of tonic with gin on the side (which you unobtrusively leave undrunk). If the bartender knows you and is tipped off in advance, he'll serve you water on ice in an old fashioned glass, which all will assume is a very dry martini on the rocks. Rum and cola (with the rum remaining in the bottle) is another possibility. At home, try varying the sweet nonalcoholic bottled beverages with a slurp of our own invention, a bastardized version of the Bull Shot which we've dubbed the Cow Shot: bouillon in a tall glass with lots of ice and a dash each of lime and Tobasco to take the place of the booze.

My girl and I were invited to spend a long weekend in the country with a married couple who lives there. We found that a third couple had also been invited. Sunday our host suggested we go out for dinner so his wife wouldn't have to do any more cooking. It seemed courteous to agree it would be fun to eat out—which we did, at a charming country inn with not-so-charming prices. What with drinks and dinner and brandy after, the check—sans tip—came to $70-plus. I suggested we split it three ways, the other male guest agreed, but our host insisted on picking up the entire tab. The next day, on the way back to town, the girl I was with wondered aloud whether I was wrong in suggesting the split, rather than gallantly reaching for the check. She felt pretty sure I should have paid, or split it with the other visitor, then or later, but that definitely our host should not have been the one to pay. I thought—and still think—she was wrong, but I'm not completely certain.—J. D., Cincinnati, Ohio.

As host, your friend had the prerogative of calling the mealtime tune. You were correct in making a verbal offer to divvy the tab—and also correct in accepting his generosity. (There's nothing more awkward than an afterdinner who-pays debate.) Your next move is to repay him in kind by inviting him and his wife to dinner in a restaurant where the cost of living it up is equally high.

I have been a widower for three years, look back on my marriage as having been a very happy one, and feel the loss of my wife with a sorrow that I believe will always endure. I tell you this so you won't think me heartless or shallow when you read what follows.

Although I was happily married, I have come to enjoy my bachelorhood and am not looking for a wife, though I am not in principle averse to remarriage. I find ample feminine companionship, of varying degrees of intimacy, and I think that for me, at this juncture in my life, variety provides the ideal spice for my days and nights. My problem is a couple with whom my late wife and I had been very friendly. They are compulsive matchmakers. I have little in common with them except the past. They invite me to dinner almost weekly, usually with eligible girls. I've yet to meet one there who was not intelligent, warmhearted, cultivated, attentive, pleasant—and sexually about as interesting as a board fence. I'm no sex fiend, but I must admit that sexually unstimulating girls bore me; for conversation I prefer the company of men. How do I get out of these invitations gracefully and without a residue of hurt feelings? —W. H., Louisville, Kentucky.

Next time you're invited, ask if you may bring a guest and take along the sexiest chick you know. Repeat, if necessary, with a new girl each time, until the cure is effected.

Three months ago I started dating a magnificent Amazon who's a dancer in the front lines at a mainstem nightery. We have a lot of laughs together and a fine physical rapport, and while she's not exactly the kind of girl I'd want to bring home to mother, for the time being life is great. Believe it or not, I'm even helping her to study philosophy. There's just one flaw in all of this: At 6'1", the girl and I stand eye-to-eye, barefoot, but with chic spike heels she is a good 3" taller than I. Needless to say, this occasions stares wherever we go. I'm beginning to wonder if I'm making an ass of myself by dating her in public. Do you feel there is something inherently ludicrous in a guy squiring a chick several inches taller than he?—S. L., New York, New York.

Of course not. If a couple gets along, the question of relative height is totally irrelevant. In all likelihood, it's not the girl's altitude that is causing all the commotion, but her good looks. So enjoy the stares—they are a compliment to you and the beauty on your arm.

My girl recently bought a sporty blue Sprite and is so nuts about it that now when we set out on a date she insists that we take her car, not mine. Not only that—she pleads with me to let *her* do the driving. I'm all for letting her have her fun and all that, but I just don't feel right sitting idly by while she works us through traffic. It bothers me—but I also realize that I may be making a mountain out of a molehill. Am I?—D. M., San Francisco, California.

No—your malaise is legitimate. While there's no harm in letting her play Jeeves once or twice, thereafter you should put yourself back in the driver's seat. Point out to her that she has ample opportunity for driving her car when she is by herself, and add that it is as improper for her to be chauffeuring you about town as it would be if she paid the check for your next night out.

At a private dinner party recently, one of the guests dropped and broke a wine glass. Immediately thereafter, our host arose from the table and ceremoniously dashed his glass in the fireplace. There were smiles all around, but I secretly felt that this performance had called attention unnecessarily to the guest's accident. Don't you agree?—R. F., Denver, Colorado.

Only in part. Your host was adhering to an Old World custom of graciousness with smashing proof that the breakage was no shattering loss. In the same situation, however, we would merely say, "Don't worry about it, Charlie," and let it go at that.

 I would like to know when it is considered proper for a guy to have his suit jacket (or sports jacket) unbuttoned. For instance, when I dine out, is it *de rigueur* that my jacket remain buttoned throughout the meal? Being a type who likes to unbend while feeding the inner man, I sincerely hope that such isn't the case. What's the story?—J. J., Philadelphia, Pennsylvania.

Sorry, J. J., but in any intrinsically social situation both suit jackets and sports jackets should normally remain buttoned. The only exception in the suit category is the vested suit, which does permit an opened jacket. It is usually acceptable to wear a sports jacket open if a sweater or vest is worn beneath. Naturally, if you're alone with friends you may suit yourself in any manner you wish. In public, though, don't loose your buttons.

 Whenever I take my girl out to dinner we have a minor set-to over the terminology I use in ordering for us. The cause of it all is the fact that she does not like being referred to as "she" (as in, "She'll have the roast beef, and I'll have duck"). According to her, this is ill-mannered and demeaning. When I ask what the hell I'm supposed to call her, she claims I should say, "my date." This I can't buy. How about it?— L. U., Denver, Colorado.

While designating your companion to a waiter as "she" is not considered really boorish in America, it is nonetheless inelegant. Referring to her as "my date" is blatant bad form. Try saying, "The lady will have . . ."—the term may not always be accurate, but it will at least impart a civilized aura to the proceedings.

Please let me know correct procedure on the following: I've always thought that a gentleman never shakes hands with a lady unless the latter proffers her hand first, but recently I've seen this rule broken. And, is hand-kissing strictly Continental or is it done on our shores, too?—S. C., Blacksburg, Virginia.

The handbook on shaking contains this rule of thumb: do whatever is most comfortable for both parties. If it's an older woman, she may cling to social graces of another era and leave the mitt pumping to the men. Never make the first move, but if the lady in question makes a meaningful gesture, be quick to respond; no one enjoys being left with an arm in a state of suspended animation. And just because the recipient of your handshake is a female, don't be afraid to make it a firm clasp (but not a bone-crusher); a dead fish still feels like a dead fish no matter what the gender on the receiving end. Hand-kissing is another matter entirely. It is not a public greeting on these shores. There is an exception; if a European married woman extends her hand with the obvious

*expectation of having it kissed, you should be prepared
to do the courteous thing, to wit: take her fingers
lightly in yours, bow slightly, and just touch the back
of her hand with your lips.*

Recently I admired a cane in a friend's house and
he very generously gave it to me. Carrying it home I
was amazed at the amount of pleasure to be had from
swinging the thing around. (This is a straight cane
of green ebony with a silver top.) I started carrying
it once in a while during the day, but everybody is
on me for it. Maybe not everybody can carry a cane,
or wear a stick, as I believe the expression used to be,
but I'm 6'4" and 210 pounds and I can and will. Don't
you think I'm right?—J. McR., Seattle, Washington.

*We would never argue with a six-four, 210-pounder
carrying a cane. There've been many epochs in the
past when the well-turned-out male would have been
thought absurdly underdressed without a walking stick.
Ditto spats. Ditto the codpiece. And there have been
many, many elegant touches from the past recently
incorporated into today's urban look, such as the cape
and the cuffed sleeve lifted directly from Edwardian
days. You, and your whangee, may be the frontrun-
ners of another style cycle. The best of British luck
to you.*

What is the protocol of the corsage? How formal
does a social occasion have to be in order to require
a corsage for my date? Do I have the florist send it
or do I take it with me? How do I know if the corsage
I select will harmonize with my girl's dress? Is it OK

to ask her what color dress she's wearing?—R. D., Buffalo, New York.

We are inclined to consider the whole corsage business as a bothersome antediluvian holdover. There are several situations, however, in which the corsage is de rigueur, and one of them is the formal dance. But even these affairs are getting less formal, and the giving of flowers more discretionary. If you insist on playing the courtly beau, here are some rules of the road. Don't go overboard; a small corsage is the safe move no matter what the size of the female or how formal the affair to which you're squiring her. Send the corsage, by all means; it's a timesaver and avoids the awkward "For me?" It's bee-oo-ti-ful!" business. It's an adventurous (and foolhardy) guy who doesn't find out the color of his girl's dress before financing the floral offering; besides, she may have an allergy and say no to flowers altogether. Incidentally, one of the posher arbiters of the social graces considers the use of the word "corsage" (instead of "flowers") as veddy plebeian, but we have nothing against the word, just the custom.

My date and I recently dined at a first-class restaurant. We were met at the door by the maître de who escorted us to our table. The captain then came over and took our drink order; the waiter served during the meal, the captain asked several times if everything was satisfactory. Whom should I have tipped and how much?—D. F., Montreal, Quebec.

It's very easy for the novice to become trapped in the largess labyrinth. Here's a handy tip sheet to follow. The waiter, naturally, gets tipped (at least fifteen percent), the captain gets nothing except a "Thank you" unless he performs some special service (and not merely taking drink orders or asking whether you enjoyed your meal), in which case the tip is a dollar or two. If the wine steward is called on, he receives fifteen percent of the wine bill or one dollar, whichever is greater, as a tip. You may tip the maître de beforehand if you desire a special table at a restaurant where you're not known. If you are a regular patron it's more appropriate to tip him as you leave; you needn't do it every time you go there, however. In either case, the tip should range from five or ten dollars in the posher places down to a minimum of one, but never silver. It is not mandatory that you tip the maître de at all.

Are there particular times when a breast-pocket handkerchief is essential? And should it be squared, pointed or just leisurely gathered? Also, is a colored handkerchief appropriate?—M. N., Miami, Florida.

The breast pocket handkerchief is always appropriate and—oftentimes—essential as well. White is the preferred color, although silk squares in neat patterns add a spark to that solid suit. As for folding, select the technique in terms of your physical type. If you're short, the pointed ends are most effective. If you're tall, try the leisurely-gathered method.

When attending a large dinner party, is it always necessary to wait until the hostess is served before starting to eat?—F. R., Charlotte, North Carolina.

Not unless you're fond of cold victuals. At dinners that include more than six guests, it is perfectly proper

129

protocol to begin eating as soon as several of the other guests—at least three or four—have also been served. Usually your hostess will give you the green light at this point anyway—but even if she doesn't, you'll be committing no faux pas in appreciatively setting to before she and the remaining guests are able to follow suit. In parties of six and under, where food service is more expeditiously accomplished, it's good form to wait until all have received their fare.

All right, please give me the straight story: what's the proper spot, in front, back, or by her side, for a gentleman when he and a young lady are (a) going up and down stairs, and (b) going up and down theatre aisles?—T. R., Hyannis Port, Massachusetts.

If a stairway is uncrowded, the lady and the gentleman ascend side by side, with the lady given the rail position. If a mob is present, the guy climbs first to clear a path. Descending, the gentleman will invariably precede his date, to offer protection should the lady stumble. Theatre-aisle protocol works like so: If you're being ushered to your seats, let the usher go first, followed by your date, while you come third. If no usher is present, you lead the foray down the aisle, with your date bringing up the rear. On the way out— if the aisle is not too crowded—take the stroll side by side; if it is jammed, you run interference.

I've just come to the conclusion that I must do something to deflate my incipient paunch. While dieting, though, I do not want to eliminate totally the pleasure of social drinking. Would you suggest to me two or three drinks that are among the lowest in calorie count, which are nonetheless potent enough to give one a lift? I know I'm going to have to give up martinis—but I don't want to be reduced to a diet cola.—T. C., Madison, Wisconsin.

First, aperitif wines such as vermouth, St. Raphael, Positano, Punt e Mes etc. Their penetrating, lingering flavors are conducive to slow sipping, and all are low in calories (four ounces of dry vermouth on the rocks contain a mere 120 calories). Second, tall drinks such as rum, bourbon or Scotch and soda or 80-proof vodka and tonic. There's less of a tendency to gulp these in the same quantities as smaller, calorie-packed cocktails or straight liquor taken neat. Finally, a bottle of stout or ale sipped before dining (about 150 calories) not only satisfies the psyche's demands of the cocktail hour but often acts as a restraining influence against later overindulgence at the table.

In a restaurant, when is it proper to send food not to your liking back to the kitchen? I'm always hesitant to complain about something I've been served, as the waiter is either embarrassingly solicitous or else he tries to give me the third degree on what was wrong with the food.—T. R., Pittsburgh, Pennsylvania.

There is a vast deluded multitude of restaurant-goers which is cowed into submissively accepting anything and everything that's brought out of the kitchen. It can be burned, raw, wrong or rancid—no matter, it will either be eaten or left for the busboy to remove. It sounds crazy, but it's done every day across the nation. There are some simple tenets to adhere to in dining out: if the food's bad, back it goes; if it's wrong, it's returned. If you want your beef rare and

131

*it's medium, send it back; if the waiter recommends
something and you don't care for it, tell him so; if it's
a decent restaurant, he'll say he's sorry for leading you
astray and will bring you something more to your liking; if it isn't a decent restaurant, what are you doing
there in the first place?*

May I wear a plain white dress shirt with regular
pointed collar under a dinner jacket? I don't dig
those lacy-ruffled formal shirts at all.—G. P., Washington, D.C.

*We don't dig lacy-ruffled formal shirts either, but
there are any number of simply-pleated formal shirts
that are correct under a dinner jacket. A plain dress
shirt is never an acceptable substitute for formalwear.*

Although I'm a country girl who recently emigrated
to the big town, I thought I had pretty well acclimated
myself to city ways—until I began dating a man who
hails taxis by waving his walking stick in the air. Isn't
this boorish?—Miss F. W., New York, New York.

*Hardly; we think it's a fine way to get a taxi—
especially in the dog-eat-dog world of Gotham cab
grabbing.*

I've been having a squabble with a young lady whom
I have been seeing regularly (though we are not engaged) for the past six months. When friends invite
us to a cocktail party, she insists it's my solemn duty
to stick by her side the entire evening. She yelps if I

so much as wander off for a minute and all hell breaks loose if I should speak to another girl when she's not around. I say she has holes in her head, that the whole *raison d'être* of a party is to get people to mix as much as possible and to make new acquaintances. Who's right, the lady or I?—T. J., Cambridge, Massachusetts.

You. Unless the party is a special occasion (dinner, going-away, birthday, wedding, etc.), the correct thing, even for married couples, is to get in there and mix it up as much as you possibly can, and this holds for the lady as well as yourself. There are few more drearily dull affairs than a party at which the same groups of people band together the whole night long, and exchange the same yawny gossip. This doesn't mean that you should ignore your date completely. Take her with you on the rounds, if you wish, but be sure to introduce yourselves to as many new faces as possible. You'd be surprised what fascinating types you can meet, just in case your six-month ladyfriend turns out to be the possessive bitch she sounds like.

My problem involves dancing. I would like to become a first-rate swinger on the dance floor; however, the lonely-heartish atmosphere and the high cost of lessons leave me less than enthusiastic about dance studios. Could you give a frustrated social hoofer a tip or two?—W. M., Cadillac, Michigan.

Your problem has a ready-made—and delightful— solution. Select a filly who seems an especially compatible armful, and—with boyish humility—explain your frustration. Chances are that she'll lend you her talents, as most girls will leap at the opportunity to aid a helpless male who wants to polish his social graces. Naturally, you'll want to start your sessions in private,

*free from intruding eyes—in your apartment, say, with
the drapes tactfully closed, and with something soft,
slow and basic on the phonograph. Who knows, you
may even learn how to dance.*

My girl and I had a violent argument recently about
revolving-door etiquette. Which is proper: Should the
man enter the door first, thereby exerting the initial
turning force, or should he stand aside allowing the
lady to go first, but also forcing her to do the pushing?
—W. H., Brooklyn, New York.

*If you had a violent argument over this, we wonder
what happens when you discuss something really important. To be correct, the man should let the woman
into the revolving door first, turn it as she goes in,
follow her in the next compartment and do all the
pushing himself.*

In a good restaurant, is a nod the proper way of
acknowledging acceptance of a wine steward's offering? Also, if the wine is poor, is it permissible to reject
it?—H. K., Flushing, New York.

*Good wine deserves more than a nod; a verbal rat-
ing of "fine" or "excellent" will stand in much better
stead than a mere bending of the neck. Poor wine
should never be accepted.*

My husband and I recently attended a large, but
not formal, dinner party, during which a speechmaker
proposed several toasts. There was some confusion as

to whether the women in the group should have stood during each toast. Some did, while others remained seated. What is correct in this situation?—Mrs. M. L., New York, New York.

If the person proposing the toast was standing—an optional position, unless a head of state is being toasted—then everyone in the company should have done likewise.

How does one refuse wine at the dinner table when the host indicates he is about to refill glasses?—C. C., Boston, Massachusetts.

By pointedly placing one's finger on the rim of one's glass. We last saw this curious ritual performed in 1947, in Des Moines.

A question of etiquette, please: I date two girls who have different opinions on whether or not I should climb first into those tunnellike cabs converted from small stock sedans. One girl says to hell with protocol, why should she squirm her way across the seat to make room for me, or have me try to climb over her after she takes her seat nearest the cab door? The other one says she'd rather put up with the discomfort than have me, her escort, look like a selfish jerk by getting in first. What to do?—F. W., New York, New York.

As you imply, if the cab's big enough, you should hold the door and help the girl in; going by the book, she should sit right down and let you climb over her to the far side of the seat. But even in big cabs this may be awkward, and current practice makes it perfectly permissible for her to slide over and make room

135

for you. We are all for the niceties, but in the matter of small cabs—especially when it's topcoat weather or the girl's in full skirt or long evening dress—we suggest this: as you open the cab door for the girl, ask her if she'd like to get in first, and be guided by her answer. If she says so, it is an extra courtesy to help her in and then go around the cab and get in the other door.

Not too long ago I had the misfortune of eating at a restaurant where the food was bad and the service impossible. Our waitress was not just slow; she was also rude, boorish and clumsy. I didn't leave a tip, much to my wife's chagrin. (She said the girl probably had a family to support, etc.) Though I don't anticipate going back, I'd like to know if you think I was justified in not leaving her so much as a dime.— R. M., Whitman, Massachusetts.

Certainly you were. If it ever happens again, you might consider leaving just one dime—to indicate clearly that your failure to tip wasn't just oversight. If she does have a family to support, she'll soon learn that her tips vary with the quality of her service.

...and
on the
go

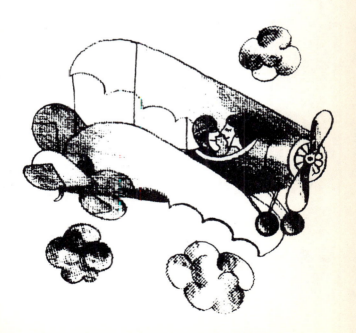

...and on the go

"for my part, i travel

not to go anywhere, but to go.

i travel for travel's sake.

the great affair is to move."

we share robert louis stevenson's wanderlust,

with the additional thought that

"a pleasant companion reduces the length

of the journey." (publilius syrus)

It's easy to find out if a prospective vacation spot is attractive, expensive, and what activities it offers, etc., but how can you determine if young, unattached people go there?—F. O'B., New Haven, Connecticut.

There are some common-sense clues which should give you a fair idea of the clientele. First, if it's a resort that specializes in sports such as skiing, on snow or water, you can be sure that the crowd is going to be young. If it's a place that bills itself as a great spot for the whole family, pitches its restful surroundings, or devotes a gread deal of its advertising or brochure space to its food, cross it off the list. Also, if a place is too expensive, it will keep away a good many chicks who can't get up the scratch. Best bet is to check with a reputable travel agent who's interested in getting your repeat business. He should be able to give you the straight scoop on what swings and what limps.

When I was in Paris a while back, I went to a movie. A charming, good-looking usher (in France, sensibly, they're women) led me to my seat. When I sat down and began watching the film, she admonished me in French, then stomped off. What was my error? —W. F., Portland, Maine.

Monsieur, you committed what ze Americans call ze botch. The fair young thing was waiting for a tip for escorting you to your seat, a custom unique to certain European countries. Whatever it was she howled in French needs no translation. Next time you're in Paris, say it with francs.

I'm going to Europe shortly and plan to buy a car when I return. I would like to know if it's true that I can save money by buying the car there, driving it around for a month or two, then bringing it back to the States.—L. D., Greenwich, Connecticut.

Yes. You'll have the advantage of cheap transportation in Europe and, because of lower import tariffs on "used" cars you can, in some instances, save enough on the purchase price to pay your round-trip jet fare. For example, a Volkswagen sedan selling for around $1640 in the U.S. can be purchased at Wolfsburg for $1302; a Jaguar XK-E roadster sells for $6100 Stateside and can be purchased at Coventry for around $4350. Make sure you rack up enough European miles *to satisfy the Customs definition of "used" (check with the manufacturer to find out how many kilometers turn your particular make into a used car) and you will save greatly on tariffs, which will run only between $60 and $200 or so, depending on the car— a saving of from $200 to $1350 over new-car tariffs. Shipping costs and European registration will add another $150 to $250, but all in all you'll still save plenty.*

■ just bought my first sports car, an MG Midget, and I have been accused by several of my more experienced driver friends of not getting the full potential out of my four-speed gearbox. For example, I always take the tachometer up to red line (6000 rpm) in first and second gears, but when I reach the legal speed limit in third—which generally occurs at about 3000 rpm—I automatically shift into high gear for cruising. Now I'm told that it would be better to stay in third gear while cruising than to shift into high before reaching 6000 rpm in third. If I were to follow this advice, I would rarely get into fourth gear under normal driving conditions. So who's right; should I always try to go to red line in each gear or continue to cruise in high gear?—M. C., St. Paul, Minnesota.

Your friends are wrong. It's pointless, wasteful of gasoline and rubber, and destructive of the engine to run a car on the red line all the time. The tachometer red line is put there to remind you that if you go much past it you are likely to blow up the engine. (In racing, a driver will run to the limit before shifting, and perhaps a couple of hundred revs over the limit, but long engine life is a factor of minimal concern in his thinking.) It is also bad practice to run a small, light engine slowly under load, but most engines of this type are happy in the band from 2000 to 4000 rpm and this is where they should be for most of the time.

Is there really any wash-and-wear suit fabric that can be worn after washing without touch-up ironing? The suits I've had have been fairly passable, but certainly not perfect, after drying.—R. L., New Orleans, Louisiana.

All wash-and-wear suits require some touch-up ironing if they are to be wrinkle-free. However, the big plus of a wash-and-wear suit is in the wearing— that is, in its resistance to wrinkling and the ability of trousers to hold a crease in hot, humid weather. But if you want your suit to be as smooth as your approach, you'd better press on regardless.

This summer, while returning from a vacation in Europe, I enjoyed a very pleasant shipboard romance with a young lady named Diana. Lately she called to say that she has just moved into an apartment here in New York. Now, for the life of me, I can't remember her last name or the address she gave me over the phone. I'm most anxious to see her again, but how can I find her?—R. K., New York, New York.

It sounds to us as though subconsciously you really want to ditch this dish, R. K. But since you insist that the spark remains, we'll try to help you find a detour around your own mental block. We assume that you know the name of the ship on which you both sailed (you do remember that, don't you?) and that you probably remember her cabin number. Even if you recall only the former, you can call the cruise line, explain your problem, and from them learn Diana's surname. Next, get in touch with the phone people and ask if they have a new phone listing under her name—even if she's a Jones girl you shouldn't have any difficulty in locating your right number, learning her address, and reestablishing relations.

I'm planning on touring Europe next year. Could you tell me what would be the best type of camera to take with me in terms of portability and ease of operation, as weighed against quality of pictures?—J. W., New Haven, Connecticut.

Your best bet would be an automatic electric-eye 35mm camera. It will do most of the work for you, is lightweight, and will take highly satisfactory shots. You can pick up a decent one for about $100.

Ten months from now I plan to set off on a once-in-a-lifetime journey: a long, leisurely trip around the world. Prior to booking accommodations, I have been assembling from books and conversations a list of the world's finest hotels. As a check to see if I've forgotten any, I'd appreciate your giving me your own selection of the 10 best—that is, the 10 hotels that offer the most luxurious accommodations in conjunction with excellence of service, excellence of site and high caliber of clientele. I want to arrange my itinerary so that I will hit as many as possible.—J. D., New York, New York.

The word "best" is, to some extent, a matter of personal preference; our choice of 10 would be drawn

*from this list: The Copacabana Palace at Rio de Janei-
ro; Claridge's in London; The Ritz in Lisbon; Estoril
Palace Hotel at Estoril; Reids at Madeira; The Palace
in Madrid; The Hostal de los Reyes Catolicos at San-
tiago de Compostela, Spain; The Formentor in Majorca;
The Crillon in Paris; The Negresco in Nice; La
Verniaz at Evian-les-Bains, France; Baur au Lac in
Zurich; The Beau Rivage in Geneva; The Excelsior
in Rome; The Ashoka in New Delhi; The Okura in
Tokyo; and the Beverly Hills Hotel in Beverly
Hills.*

My boss and his wife have invited me and my
fiancée to be their sole guests for a week-long cruise
on their modest yacht. Would it be correct for me to
offer to supply either food or liquor?—H. L., New
London, Connecticut.

*Yes. You can offer to add to the larder or supply
the booze; if it's a powerboat, you can also offer to
pay for the fuel. And after the cruise, of course, a
bread-and-butter gift is mandatory.*

For over a year I have enjoyed a very intimate and
highly satisfactory relationship with an eligible and
knowledgeable bachelor. Although I have handled myself to his satisfaction in public so far, I would like
your suggestions about a situation that will arise soon.
We expect to spend several long weekends vacationing
together at resorts. He obviously knows the proper
hotel procedure for a legally unattached couple. However, being a girl with a rather cloistered background,
I don't. Since my behavior to date has led him to

believe that I can conduct myself in a discreet and circumspect manner, I don't want to shatter this illusion by asking *him* for advice.—C. J., Albany, New York.

This seems to be much ado about very little. After the two of you register for separate rooms, we suggest you conduct yourself in public in a manner best suited to a girl very much taken with the man in her life; we're sure your escort plans to return the compliment. Your private lives, as in the past, should be nobody's business but your own.

'm headed for a short stay at Ocho Rios, Jamaica, and plan to take along my Bermuda shorts. When wearing them, what determines the length of one's socks? Is it simply a function of temperature, or what?— H. B., Augusta, Maine.

No, it's a function of activity. Knee-high socks should be donned after five o'clock when a jacket is worn with the shorts. Socks of mid-calf length should be worn for informal daytime doings. Short socks should be reserved for active sports wear. Incidentally, rather than pack your shorts you might wait to buy a couple of pairs on the island itself, where an excellent local product is available in the popular Jamaican length.

On a recent ten-day cruise my companion and I were unable to get a table for two and found ourselves placed with four strangers. I enjoy a bottle of wine over dinner, and felt rather antisocial not offering to share same with our tablemates. But I reasoned that offering to share would have placed them under obligation to reciprocate, when they actually might not wish to do so. I'm planning a similar cruise shortly, and I'd like to know if I goofed.—D. Q., Los Angeles, California.

You did. You felt rather antisocial because, after all, refusing to share wine with four tablemates is rather an antisocial act. When the table is small enough to permit easy conversation among all guests, you should offer your wine around. If your hospitality is accepted, your tablemates will reciprocate in kind at a later meal. If rejected, no obligations are incurred, and you and your companion can proceed to imbibe guiltlessly. In either case, the result is good will— rather than unpleasant afterthoughts.

During the summer months I like to wear short-sleeved dress shirts. This creates a problem, however; when I wear a sports jacket (which naturally has had its sleeve length tailored to show some shirt cuff) it looks like I've either outgrown the jacket or it's shrunk. Do I have to sacrifice comfort for looks?— D. B., Detroit, Michigan.

Although approximately 70 percent of summer shirts sold today are short-sleeved, you'll be more correctly garbed if you switch to long-sleeved dress shirts in featherweight warm-weather fabrics; a bare wrist poking out of a jacket sleeve is liable to give you an adolescent "my-how-that-boy-is-shooting-up" look.

The crowd I go with is making plans for a ski week-end, and I'm hung up. I am strictly an indoor man and don't know the first thing about slaloms and her-ringbones. Should I chicken out, or try to bluff my way through?—R. B. G., Pittsburgh, Pennsylvania.

You really don't have to do either. Let's face it; you just can't fake skiing. And we don't advise phonying an accident, either. Your cohorts won't believe it. Even if they do, the only thing you'll get out of it is a solo stint in the ski lodge. First thing to do is to de-termine just how proficient your crowd is. If there are a number of novices to keep you company on the beginners' slope, then there's no need to bluff; going to school with a flock of snow bunnies can be fun. If they're at the intermediate level or better, your wisest move might be to defer accepting any invitations until you've gone to ski school on your own and feel you can make a respectable showing. Of course, if you're a man completely given to urban pursuits, why fight your natural instincts? Indoor amusements have a non-seasonal attraction that avoids both frostbite and sunstroke.

Recently I asked a young lady of my acquaintance if she would care to spend a weekend with me in Las Vegas. She seemed delighted at the idea and replied that she would be more than happy to be my guest. Then, after I had bought a pair of plane tickets and was about to telegraph for a room reservation, she advised me that, of course, it was going to be separate quarters. I now regret having asked her—but I don't know how to back out gracefully. What would be a suitable course of action in a situation such as this?—B. B., New York, New York.

Honor your word and go. A weekend invitation of this sort does not necessarily imply a blanket situation as well, and if the young lady wants to sleep solo she has every right to do so. The fact that you are paying the freight in no way entitles you to a rounder-trip ticket. Our hunch is that her acceptance of the invitation and her insistence on the proprieties of separate accommodations imply a desire to maintain appearances coupled with a tacit willingness to be persuaded once you're on the scene. If your gambling instincts don't go beyond the gaming tables, however, we suggest you research your prospective traveling companions a bit more throughly in the future, and thus avoid any chance of disappointments.

A coed has invited me to join her and three sorority sisters for a weekend at their summer pad on the dunes of East Hampton. I have accepted, of course, but am struck with this thought: When a man joins a woman for a weekend of surfing who pays what bills?—R. S., New York, New York.

Follow the rules laid down for campus vacations. You pay your own transportation, of course, and it is appreciated (but not required) if you take your date a present. If you're staying at her hut, you'd better be prepared to split the food and liquor bills during your stay. If not, your coed has probably reserved a room for you at a hotel (which you should pay for) or with friends. If it is the latter, take along a gift for the hostess, but don't volunteer to buy staples (it's considered de trop).

The thing I hate about ski weekends is ski pros. Not only do they manhandle your girls on the instruction slopes, they also make a play for them later on in the lounges below. My question is this: When the ski pro, in the guise of camaraderie, sits down at my table and eyes my girl, am I obliged to pay for his drink?—L. C., Denver, Colorado.

It's up to you. At ski lodges it's tacitly assumed that fraternizing with the guests is a legitimate part of the ski pro's job; being in general a friendly and fun-loving lot, and heroes in their element, these gents are frequently not above capitalizing on the situation for make-out purposes. If a conning pro joins you and your girl, you can offer to buy him a drink or indicate that you're involved in a private conversation and you'll be happy to see him on the slopes next morning—either course is considered polite. As in all other occupations that are staffed by single young athletes, the ski-instructor dodge has its share of pushy boors. However, the majority of instructors are sensitive to the fact that they are part hero and part hired help, and are quick to detect a hint that they are intruding.

When you are checking out of one of the better hotels after a longish stay, which of the help do you tip and how much?—K. P., Greenwich, Connecticut.

If it's American plan and you've not been paying cash for food, and have been signing chits for drinks and other extras, your best bet is to ask the management to distribute gratuities for you and turn over to them for this purpose an amount equal to one day's tariff per week of your stay. This is increasingly customary. Some hotels, especially in tropical resort areas, automatically provide a list of those employees who have served you directly, with suggested gratuity per week for each. In our experience, these suggestions

*run a bit high, and spending a goodly part of your last
day setting aside packets of earmarked bills is a drag,
so we prefer the lump-sum-to-management procedure.
The same system can be followed in European-plan
places, but the total pelf and number of deserving
recipients will be less.*

This summer I went on a charter cruise (no crew)
with a close friend and his new wife. He had to inter-
rupt the vacation to plane back to his office for a day.
About the time we expected him back, the tender of
the yacht club where we were lying on a guest moor-
ing came out to give us the message that my friend
had called and said he'd have to spend the night in
town because weather had grounded his return flight.
We didn't doubt it: within an hour it was pouring,
with much thunder and lightning. It was very cozy and
intimate in the close quarters below; we were burning
a candle to save the battery and—to put it euphemis-
tically—romance took the helm. It was clear and
bright in the morning, but my conscience wasn't. My
friend showed up in time for brunch and the rest of
the cruise went well superficially, but I had a nagging
feeling he gradually wised up to the indiscretion that
occurred while he was away. Nothing was said, but
I felt that searching looks were exchanged. I've
avoided the couple in the weeks since. Yesterday, the
wife called me at my office—the first time we talked
alone since that night—and said she was sure I shared
her feelings of guilt and remorse, but that I was making matters worse, and arousing suspicion, by shunning
our erstwhile socializing. I was saved, for the nonce,
by a two-month business trip to Latin America—a
wonderful last-minute reprieve which made it possi-

ble to say my *auf Wiedersehens* by phone. But this thing hangs over me and I don't know what my future course should be when I return. You may think me a louse, but I maintain that there is no reason for me to give up a meaningful friendship because of one night of unreason—which I can't find it in my heart to completely regret. How do I handle this mess on my return?—P. G., San Francisco, California.

Don't carry your remorse code too far—unless you're getting some kind of reverse pleasure out of punishing yourself. Remember, it's often better to feel remorse for what you've done than to feel regret for what you failed to do. Remember, also, the words of a fine old ditty: "It takes two to tango." If the wife can live with this memory, you can, too. Better yet, forget it; if you and your friends can stay friends, then do so. If it doesn't work out, you can coolly cool it until the relationship fades away just as surely as your feelings of guilt are bound to.

■'m planning a trip to England this year and want to dress right. I'm all set except for one thing: I don't know the difference between regimental striped ties and rep striped ties. Is there any? If so, where can I obtain the more authentic type?—D. B., Raritan, New Jersey.

Regimental stripes are diagonal, their width and colors varying according to the old British Army regiments they represent. Rep (also repp) is a material from which diagonally striped ties are generally made in America. The stripes follow no uniform pattern, nor do the colors. If you search hard, you can probably find imitation regimental stripes (as well as old school and club ties) in local haberdasheries, but we advise you not to wear them on your trip abroad. Should you be wandering about London sporting a cravat belonging to a regiment in which you have not served, there is a fair chance some elderly English gentleman will land you a smartish clout on the mazard with his walking stick.

I'm planning a trip to London shortly, and while there wish to have a suit made by a tailor highly recommended by a friend. I want something I can wear inconspicuously in London, but which I can also wear home without looking like an unreconstructed Tory. Can you give me suggestions?—J. C., Charleston, South Carolina.

We assume you want a predominantly British look, or you wouldn't be going to a London tailor in the first place. British tailors are geniuses at suiting the individual individually, and to benefit fully from their skills you should follow closely their recommendations as to style, fabric and cut. If you acquiesce in the traditional long lapels and double vents, you can still preserve your Yankee integrity by watching waist suppression and lapel width, two areas where British conservatism tends to evaporate.

During a two-week vacation in the Bahamas recently, I encountered a unique situation: While indulging in some early morning scuba diving I spotted a strikingly beautiful young girl engaged in a similar pursuit—sans bikini. After three mornings of coincidental path-crossing we met, discovered that we shared many interests besides early A.M. dips. For the rest of our stay, we had a ball. So, when she made ready to leave the hotel, I volunteered to pay her bill and she accepted the offer. We separated with a promise to see each in the near future but I can't help thinking that I should not have picked up her hotel tab. Was this a sucker move on my part?—J. Y., Washington, D.C.

It was certainly generous, that's for sure. But if the two weeks with your mermaid were as pleasant as you describe, we'd never call you a patsy. Still, you have established a precedent with her and you'll have to cuff your next jaunt together unless you tell her otherwise in advance.

Two friends and I are going on a long hunting weekend in the woods of Maine. The cabin we'll be staying in has a small stove, but no refrigerator. What provisions would you suggest we take with us, that will provide simple-to-prepare, varied fare? Naturally, we hope to supplement our menu with fresh game, but on the chance that we draw a complete blank in that department we'd like to have something besides canned pork-and-beans to fall back on. Any tips?—L. B., New York, New York.

No problem—just visit a fine gourmet shop (Charles & Co. or Macy's in your city) and stock up on a wide assortment of exotic canned comestibles. You'll find everything from Swedish or Danish meat balls to clam cakes to enchiladas in sauce—the choice of victuals for a wilderness fare-thee-well is almost endless. Something else you might check out at your sporting-goods store (if portability is a problem) is Armour's Star Lite outdoor foods prepared by a freeze-drying process which removes 99 percent of their moisture. The foods need no refrigeration and keep up to two years, requiring only soaking in water before cooking to restore their moisture. There are currently 12 varieties available ranging from a ranch-style breakfast (four eggs, pork-sausage patties and fried potatoes) to shrimp creole.

In a few months, I plan to head for Switzerland to get in as much skiing as I can in six weeks. A friend has been telling me that I can't depart without taking shots against cholera, typhus, lockjaw and typhoid. True?—R. S., Baton Rouge, Louisiana.

No. Inoculations for the diseases your friend cites aren't necessary for western European jaunts. The U.S. Government requires nothing save a smallpox vaccination on your return; for the sake of convenience, most Americans heading for the Continent take care of it before they leave home. It's good for three years —but you must obtain a certificate for the health authorities here and abroad.

In the South Seas I had a fantastic wine called kava. Can you tell me more about it?—M. H., Syracuse, New York.

This potent Polynesian potable is not strictly a wine, since it's not fermented. It's made of the roots of a South Sea pepper plant, which are pounded, soaked in water and strained. (At one time the roots were chewed by virgins and then spat into coconut shells —a technique no longer followed, perhaps because of the lack of qualified personnel.) Not generally available in the U.S., kava tastes like peppery soap-

153

suds, tends to numb the mouth and throat, and if taken liberally will affect the legs but leave the mind clear. Apparently, it produces no unpleasant after-effects.

My playmate has given me an imported wicker picnic basket set that fits into the back of my Jaguar. So, I'm expressing my thanks by taking her on a picnic. It may as well be a first-cabin affair. What would you say should be the menu?—P. Y., Bronxville, New York.

To go with the Jag and picnic basket, go with an aristocratic British-type picnic menu:

Gimlet Cocktails

Pâté of Smoked Rainbow Trout
Fresh Malossal Beluga Caviar
Crackers

Cold Grilled Deviled Ringneck Pheasant
Cold Fresh Asparagus Vinaigrette

Chambertin

Stilton Cheese
Apple Tarts

Hot French Roast Coffee

Irish Mist Liqueur

decor
and decorum
in the lair

decor and decorum
in the lair

"the art of loving," said goethe,

"is like every other art . . .

it must be learned and practiced

and with incessant care."

with this in mind,

we set forth the following advice

on how to arrange the lair

for gracious living and zestful loving.

An ex-girlfriend recently showed up at my pad—unexpected and a little high. She entered the apartment (by means of the key I had let her keep as a souvenir of happier days) and surprised me *flagrante delicto* with my latest flame, who is now furious. I'm convinced this whole sorry incident was no fault of mine, and would like to learn how I can convince her of same.—L. W., Knoxville, Tennessee.

But it was your fault—for giving the key in the first place and for not demanding that she turn it in when she checked out of the club. Your move now

*is to explain to your latest that the key to the prob-
lem was nothing more than a memento. You should
underscore your words by changing your pad lock.
Chances are she'll eventually come round, because it's
difficult for girls to resist the guy who has other chicks
beating on his door—provided the latter can't get in.*

My bachelor apartment is stereo-equipped. I must
admit immodestly that the feminine traffic is heavy.
Usually, we mix a few drinks and I put some music
on the rig and, well, one thing leads to another. My
problem is this: I don't own any *complete* LPs that
are first-rate mood builders. Several tracks may be just
right, but the record makers seem to feel variety's a
virtue (which it may be, under other circumstances),
so a mood track is often followed by uptempo and
jump stuff that puts me right back at the starting line.
Either that, or I have to pop up every few minutes to
hunt for a fresh sound. This, too, does more toward
mashing the mood than the music does toward building it up. Should I just let the records keep playing
after my favorite mood-sustaining specials are over, or
continue with what I'm doing, or what?—H. W., New
York, New York.

*Neither. Get yourself a tape deck and tape your
tempting tracks in sequence. Since you're obviously
more interested in background music than in the
highest of fi for undistracted listening, use the 3¾
or 1⅞ inches-per-second speed, which should give
you enough fidelity to suit your divided attention and
enough time to unfreeze any woman. As an alternative, pick up copies of discs designed for those cozy
hours. On the pop vocal side, try Frank Sinatra's
"Only the Lonely," "No One Cares" or "In the Wee*

*Small Hours" (all on Capitol), Peggy Lee's "Pretty
Eyes" (Capitol) and Julie London's "Around Midnight" (Liberty). On the pop instrumental slant, sam-
ple the Jackie Gleason ork sides (Capitol)—several
with the glowing trumpet of Bobby Hackett featured
—or the Paul Weston discs, including "Music for
Dreaming" and "Music for Romancing" (Capitol).
For classical backgrounds, select the interpretation of
your choice from these aides d'amour: Ravel's "La
Valse" and "Pavanne pour un Infante defunte," and
Samuel Barber's "Adagio for Strings." For late-night
quiet jazz, hear a ballad set by trumpeter Chet Baker,
simply titled "Chet" (Riverside), a balladic tour by
trumpeter Roy Eldridge and strings, "That Warm
Feeling" (Verve) and guitarist Johnny Smith's "Easy
Listening" (Roost). Head for your record shop—to
collect them, and others like them, for those long,
long enchanted evenings of reaping the fruits of your
forethought.*

■'m moving into a new apartment soon and plan to
revise my system of arranging books (I have far too
many, but hate to part with a single volume). I'm a
neat type, and fairly organized, but I haven't evolved
a really satisfactory method of classification. I've tried
keeping books alphabetically by author, but this system
breaks down with picture and art books, anthologies,
poetry collections, etc. I've tried group classification
(poetry, fiction, history, biography, etc.) and alphabetical order by authors within each classification, but
there are always borderline books which defy all categories—and I get bogged down and forget my categories if there are too many of them. I like to be able
to lay my hand on a book I want without consulting

a card file. Any suggestions at all—please!—R. E., Tucson, Arizona.

If you become a compulsive organization man about your possessions, you'll be turning what should be leisure enjoyment into tedious work. We don't see any great harm in having a shelf of unmatched books (there's something a bit sterile and forbidding about a pad that carries orderliness to an excess)—but if you feel impelled to classify, the following ground rules should suffice. Start with broad group classifications—fiction, poetry, history, biography, art, etc. Arrange fiction alphabetically by author (but not painstakingly so—whether Faulkner precedes or follows Fleming doesn't matter a whit, as long as you know in which general area a book is located). We see no point in alphabetizing the volumes within your other main categories; these will probably be smaller in extent, and, after all, it doesn't take much time to scan 20 or 30 titles when searching for a particular one. Reserve a necessary number of shelves for those books which defy categorization and lump them in your mind under the title of miscellany; if these books are for use and not for show, you will be familiar with their shapes and contents and be able to select among them without undue fumbling.

I have been dating a girl who absolutely refuses to touch a drop of liquor. She's a good kid, but has never really learned how to relax and enjoy herself. Now, I have a hunch that beneath her pretty but prim exterior there lies a reservoir of warmth and affection—my problem is how to tap it. The other day I had a brainstorm. Why not try loosening her up by feeding her a meal wherein all the courses are prepared with alcoholic ingredients? I would appreciate it if you'd supply me with a menu that meets this somewhat offbeat requirement. I am a fairly accomplished cook. —A. U., Boston, Massachusetts.

Don your bonnet de chef, and rustle up the following haut fare:

> *Brandied cheddar spread*
> *Cheese soup with ale*
> *Frogs legs Provençale (white wine)*
> *Veal scaloppine Marsala*
> *Fruit-stuffed avocado, rum dressing*
> *Crepes with curaçao*
> *Cafe Brulot (cognac)*

All of the above dishes may be found in Food and Drink Editor Thomas Mario's "The Playboy Gourmet." We might add, A. U., that while your scheme is imaginative, the chances of your girl becoming even slightly high from this fine repast are slight. Whenever liquor or wine is cooked—that is, heated until it boils —the alcohol vaporizes, and the alcoholic content of the uncooked items listed here is so minute as to have no inebriating effect whatever. We suggest you rely on other, subtler factors to thaw your girl's proper façade: the appeal that the tastefully prepared viands and potables will have to her latent sensuality, and the obvious fact that you have gone out of your way to give her a pleasurable evening.

What's the straight scoop regarding the proper storage of wine? I live on the 20th floor of an apartment building and am fresh out of damp, cobwebby cellars.—B. P., New York, New York.

A wine "cellar" need not, of course, be situated in one's basement; the term applies to any storage space wherein wine is kept undisturbed. The major requisite of such a space is a steady temperature. In a modern apartment house with 20 stories or more, chances are that your least-frequently opened closet will provide a sufficiently even temperature. Ideally, this should be between 55° and 60° F., but moderate differences above or below this range will not be harmful to the vino, if the temperature remains constant. A wine cellar should also be dry, well-ventilated and kept as clean as possible to prevent the occurrence of odors and mold. Place your white wines (which are the most delicate) in the coolest spot (almost always closest to the floor), put burgundies above the whites, and bordeaux on top. All bottles should be stored on their sides so that the cork stays wet; this prevents crumbling, keeps the seal airtight and forestalls spoilage. For further details on the care and augmentation of wine cellars, check the chapter entitled "Verities of Vino" in "The Playboy Gourmet."

I'm planning to throw a large dinner party in my apartment. My girlfriend wants to act as hostess but she's afraid that it will give the impression we're living together and I'm afraid it might give her the notion she's just a license fee away from becoming a bride. Is there a rule governing this?—N. K., Charlotte, North Carolina.

If the little lady wants to lend a hand, that's commendable; an assist from the opposite sex can be very helpful when you're playing the host. You can get your female friend off the hook, if she's worried about wagging tongues, by seeing that she makes an early departure. If it's mutually agreeable, she can come back later on, after the tumult and the shouting dies, and help you stack glassware, empty ashtrays and share a nightcap. She'll have avoided gossip and you'll have neatly side-stepped giving her a mental image of eternal togetherness engendered by the picture of the two of you waving tandem farewells to departing guests.

My FM multiplex adapter is giving me fits. I receive all the FM stations in my area—including those broadcasts in multiplex—quite clearly. However, there is little separation between channels on certain stereo broadcasts, in spite of the undistorted reception. I have been coupling my FM tuner with a TV antenna. Do you think this is the problem?—R. L. M., Menlo Park, California.

No, we don't. The wrong antenna is sometimes responsible for distortion, in which case a special FM type would be required. But you say your reception is clear. You ought to check whether your multiplex adapter and tuner are properly matched. If that isn't the problem, go to a hi-fi store and listen to multiplex broadcasts on one of their systems. If they lack separation, too, it may be the fault of the broadcasting stations. Finally, it may be time for a thorough bench check of your amplifier.

Is it acceptable to offer a guest a pipe from your own rack for an after-dinner smoke? Is it acceptable to ask to borrow one?—J. O., Heidelberg, Germany.

Pipes, like toothbrushes, are neither borrowed nor lent. Back in the old days the proper host kept a supply of clay pipes on hand for his guests, to be used once and then thrown away. These are still obtainable, and,

as a host, you can offer them. As a guest, it's never
proper to request a pipe. If you don't bring your own
favorite briar when you step out to dinner, you'll have
to settle for a postprandial cigar or cigarette.

A short while ago, I started dating the girl in the
next apartment, a delectable redhead who lives with
her sweet, widowed mother. Our relationship so far
has been one big frustration. The mother's always
home—she's a TV nut who keeps a twenty-four-hour
vigil in front of the home screen. We live in a new
apartment house where the walls are tissue-paper thin.
And Mama has ears like sonar. She can even tell when
my sinuses are acting up, let alone whether I've got
her darling daughter next door. Please help me find
a solution before I retire to a monastery.—B. L., New
York, New York.

If Mums is as bugged on TV as you say, the solu-
tion might very well lie in the problem. It's a fairly
simple proposition to get her tickets for the live eve-
ning TV shows, and the later they're on the better.
The dear woman will think you're a prince of a fellow,
since no TV fanatic can resist the opportunity of see-
ing a favorite in the flesh. And while she is, you can
be, too.

I have a fine studio apartment—equipped with good
stereo, records, paintings, etc.—which I like to show
off to an appreciative audience. But how do you go
about inviting a girl to your pad on the first or second
date (after dinner, a show or the like) without telling
her all about it or making her think that your inten-

tions are bed-wise, which may (but not necessarily) be the case?—S. D., Queens Village, New York.

Invite her over for a tête-à-tête dinner before going out. Otherwise, use the record ploy: discuss tastes in music and then invite her up to hear her favorite circular etchings. If your pad is all you say it is and if you don't come on like Mr. Hyde, you should have no trouble getting her back for a second visit. In fact, you may have trouble keeping her out.

I'm sure that other bachelors have been troubled by this problem—one that I've never been able to solve satisfactorily. Whenever I'm entertaining a young lady *à deux* in my apartment, it seems that the phone rings and at the other end of the wire is invariably another young lady wanting to talk. What's the best way to ease out of this situation, without letting either girl in on it?—J. B., Chicago, Illinois.

When you escort a young lady into your apartment, for an evening of your own design, nothing should intrude. Turn down the bell on your phone (in both bedroom and living room) in advance, so it doesn't jar you or your companion. And if it rings, just gaze at the girl and murmur, "No matter who it is, it can't be more important than you," and don't answer it. The miss you're with will be delightfully flattered. The chick doing the phoning will think you're out, so she won't be bugged by visions of you and a competitor in an intimate situation.

In the past, some of the parties I've thrown have been so successful that it has taken Herculean efforts to get all the guests on their way home. For future reference, can you suggest an easy method to speed the guests who linger too long after the stated departure time?— L. K., Mineola, New York.

We don't look favorably on parties with a "stated departure time," and, so it seems, neither do your guests. Most successful parties have a way of resolving themselves naturally, without any prodding by the host. However, one sure way to dry up the hangers-on is to close the bar and suggest that everyone go out for breakfast.

Must I wear a dinner jacket when my wife wears a long hostess gown?—R. B., Mystic, Connecticut.

Depends on the occasion. If you're entertaining formally at home, you should dress formally. The vagaries of women's fashions, however, permit your wife to wear a full-length hostess gown on semi-formal occasions that do not call for formal men's attire; on these less-formal evenings, you may wear a dark (preferably black) suit.

I have two questions: Is there a proper way to open a champagne bottle (I become all thumbs when called upon to separate cork from bottle); and must a towel be wrapped around the bottle in order to serve it correctly?—W. G., White Plains, New York.

Opening a champagne bottle is a fairly simple operation. First, remove the wire and foil; hold the cork with one hand, the bottle with the other. Then (and here's the gimmick) twist the bottle gently until the cork comes out with a discreet but discernible pop.

165

The towel around the bottle is partly functional, partly custom. Years ago, when bottling was not nearly the science it is today, there was a chance that the bottle might explode in one's hands as one tried to work the cork out; the towel acted as a shield. Today, the towel's sole function is to absorb the moisture picked up from the ice bucket.

Do a few favorite antique items have an appropriate place in an apartment that's furnished in a basically contemporary manner?—N. S., Salt Lake City, Utah.

Of course. The clean, functional lines of your modern furniture will be neatly accented by the presence of more rounded and ornamented pieces from earlier periods.

The joker I share an apartment with says it's wrong to decant wine before serving it. I say it doesn't make any difference, except that a good-looking Swedish decanter adds to the general air of the table. Who's right?—R. F. J., New York, New York.

You're both right. As a general rule it's best form to serve table wine in the bottle, so that your guests can note what they're drinking without having to ask the host. Sherry, port, madeira, marsala and liqueurs are usually served in a decanter for the reason you cite, and because vintage, vineyard and so on don't matter too much. Wines that form sediment are stored, brought to table in a serving basket, and poured in near-horizontal posture, since standing them up would disturb the sediment and cloud the wine, and storing vertically would dry out the cork and admit air. To decant these wines, bottles should first be stood up for twelve to twenty-four hours to allow the sediment to settle in the bottom. Then decant slowly all but the last half inch or so which, being sedimentary dregs, should not be decanted or drunk. Some purists shudder at this, but a respectable number of connoisseurs decant their reds—even the very best—through a glass funnel lined with filter paper (the kind that is commonly available for glass coffee makers). This clears the wine of dregs and, they claim, reduces tannic astringency while permitting the wine to "breathe." Whether "breathing"—leaving the wine open to the air for about a half hour before drinking—actually improves its taste or is merely a ritual nicety has yet to be scientifically determined.

As a confirmed bachelor, I am free from many of the problems married men endure, knock wood, but there's one unique to bachelorhood of which I'm becoming increasingly aware. As the years have passed, more and more of my contemporaries have established homes and families. Our friendships have not abated; on the contrary, I am that ever-scarcer social commodity, the extra man. Accordingly, I have several dinner invitations a week, at the homes of friends. I am no chef and my studio apartment does not lend itself to reciprocal invitations to dine. I do give cocktail parties from time to time, to which I invite those to whom I'm socially obligated, but they are not elaborate enough for me to feel my social books are balanced. I've tried an occasional dinner out, where I host several couples at a restaurant. These dinners are expensive, not especially festive, and have a kind of cold impersonality about them which satisfies neither me nor my guests. I know I don't *have* to do more than I do, but I'd like to. The question is, what?—G. R., Boston, Massachusetts.

Laudable intention—not hard to fulfill. Find a caterer who can turn your cocktail parties into buffet dinners with special one-dish meals. Since you live in a large enough city, you can rapidly make a reputation for gala buffets by exploring the range of ethnic cuisine, for most foreign restaurants either offer or can steer you to home-catered buffets. You can serve, sequentially, a New Orleans oyster pan roast, a Pacific-style barbecue, an Indian curry wagon, a Spanish paella, etc.—with the caterer supplying not only food and servants, but all the extra crockery, glassware, etc., that you need.

My refrigerator-made ice cubes are usually opaque and milky. How can I get the crystal-clear cubes you see in bars?—G. P., Elkhart, Indiana.

Minerals or other impurities are one cause of milky ice cubes. In cities with reasonably clear tap water, however, the most frequent cause is the entrapment—during freezing—of minute air bubbles. The colder the water, the more of these bubbles are apt to form. Try filling your cube trays with tepid water. Hot might work better to insure clear ice, but it would take too long to freeze and might melt the ice in adjoining trays.

Ever since I gave my girl a duplicate key to my apartment, she has been gradually killing me with kindness. More often than not, I will come home from the office and find her in the process of cooking some sumptuous repast—really knocking herself out in my kitchen. She even goes through the pipe-and-slippers routine. She insists I just relax, won't let me do a thing around the apartment, cleans up after me, fluffs up the pillow in back of my head, etc. All I have to do is mention something that needs doing, and she becomes a messenger-errand girl. She has never mentioned the subject of marriage, although it is implied in her every action. She is a beautiful, intelligent, passionate girl and highly sensitive. What can I do to curtail her activities on what she thinks is my behalf and still not do anything to hurt her?—G. B., Philadelphia, Pennsylvania.

Hire a houseman who will pre-empt the duties your girl is presently undertaking. You can explain it to her as a thoughtful move on your part to take the menial tasks off her hands, leaving her free for more uplifting pursuits. Once she comes to realize that your affections are not based on her housewifely abilities, she should be more than happy to keep things on a strictly social footing. And may we add what may seem a gratuitous suggestion? Should either marriage or a bust-up fracture this particular romance, don't ever again give anyone but a domestic worker a duplicate key to your digs. For when you do, as you may already suspect, you sacrifice the freedoms of bachelorhood without gaining the benefits of connubiality. And things can only get stickier, or more marital, as time goes on.

You may find this a little difficult to believe, but I'm throwing a cocktail party next month to which I plan to invite at least half a dozen young things who I know have rarely, if ever, taken a drink. If it's proper, I'd like to offer wine in addition to cocktails. I'd appreciate your suggestions.—N.L., Wappingers Falls, New York.

Assuming that all the girl scouts in the troop are at least 18, we do find it a little difficult to believe. However, as a substitute for cocktails you can serve chilled dry sherry, dry champagne, or even a dry white wine such as moselle. You might also stock up on milk, or consider finding a new half-dozen party dolls.

When I have guests over for dinner or a midnight supper, I know the basic rule for choosing what wines to go with what dishes, but I'm still in the dark about when I should trot out an American wine and when an imported one. Can you help?—N. N., Toledo, Ohio.

The general rule is this: the best imported dinner wines (from France or Germany) are almost always superior to the best American wines; on the other hand, an inexpensive imported wine is frequently inferior to an American wine of comparable price. When you have special guests in for an elegant spread, you'll want to serve nothing but a first-rate imported wine—if for no other reason than the kudos which attaches to it—but don't plan on paying much less than five dollars a bottle. Additional suggestions: find a knowledgeable wine merchant, discuss your needs with him and rely on his advice concerning importers and vintage years. Then read the chapter entitled "The Verities of Vino" in "The Playboy Gourmet" to brush up on your basics. But always, in the last analysis, trust your own palate concerning wines. Incidentally, American wines can be delightful when you plan on dining less formally, or for brunch—and, of course, they're usually less expensive, too.

Which wines should be chilled?—K. R., West Redding, Connecticut.

Red wines are almost invariably served at room temperature, and for the rest, the general rule is the sweeter the wine the cooler it should be. White and rosé wines should be chilled (one to three hours in the refrigerator is enough), while sparkling wines should be served at near-freezing temperatures. But be careful not to overchill, or to chill for too long—because either will impair flavor and bouquet.

A very special young lady and I have been seeing each other for quite a spell now, and we've spent some delightful hours together at my apartment. Recently, though, she asked me if I'd mind if she brought over some of her own lounging attire, since my stuff is much too large for her. I don't want her gear hanging in my closet when she's not here, for obvious reasons. How can I say no—gently?—B. D., Cadillac, Michigan.

Surprise her with a gift—a man's robe and slippers in the smallest available size—and assure her that they're for her and her alone. Most women get a kick out of wearing men's duds, and these items don't stand out when hanging in your closet. And, of course, they can be used for any other emergency situation you might run into.

Lately I've been picking up the local FM station on my stereo record player. Even though the sound is faint, it does interfere with the enjoyment of my records. The volume, balance and tone controls don't seem to have any effect on it at all. Could you please

171

explain this phenomenon and give me a solution?—
J. B., Fontana, Wisconsin.

The trouble is probably caused by alternating-current lines running parallel to, and too close to, your speaker leads or other unshielded cables. If you can't separate your leads from, or make them run at right angles to, your AC lines, use shielded wires, twist them together, and ground the shields. A common "cure" is reversing your amplifier's power-cord plug in the wall socket, but we put the word cure in quotes because it seldom works.

and
so
to bed

and so to bed

the bed and its pleasures

have been praised by countless men.

even napoleon once swore

he would not exchange the joys of his

"for all the thrones in the world."

concurring with his enthusiasm for

a sumptuous haven,

we offer the following guides

to bedding down with eyes open—or closed.

My current girl is a lovely 18-year-old who is the answer to a bachelor's prayer. She cooks, she sews, she chats, she loves—and I keep coming back for more. One problem, though: The girl is somewhat hipped on self-expression and honesty, and has thought nothing of telling all and sundry among our friends and acquaintances that we two have a splendid relationship in the sack. The other night, for example, she chilled the atmosphere at a cocktail party by brightly remarking that one reason I am so wonderful is because I never snore or keep her awake at night with tossing and turning. I like flattery as well as the next guy, but not this kind, delivered in front of six virtual strangers. When I reprimanded her, she sulked and accused me of being ashamed of our relationship. Of course I'm not—but neither do I want it broadcast all over town. Any suggestions on how to gently button her pretty lip?—P. B., New York, New York.

Tell her that with big-girl pleasures go big-girl responsibilities, among which is the use of intelligent discretion. Tell her, too, that a successful relationship is one in which each partner has an honest regard for the honest needs and wants of the other—and that your own wants and needs include keeping private pleasures private. And if she still insists on broadcasting details of your amour, you may find some consolation in the thought that it pays to advertise: another female or two may catch this chatter about your intimacies and become curious. Making that point to your girlfriend might well turn the trick. Remember, when she talks openly about sharing your bed, it isn't because she's "proud" of your relationship—she simply gets an extra kick from this more public flaunting of the sexual taboos that were established for her when she was younger.

My fiancé and I have had sexual relations for over three years. At first we were satisfied with one position. Soon he suggested a new one and then a variety. Within a month of weekends (we're separated during the week), I soon found myself wanting and needing this variety for excitement. We got to the point where we wouldn't leave the room and would ring room service for food. Then it was out of bed and onto the floor or in the shower. We were constantly finding new ways

175

and places to excite each other, most of them shocking at first, but at the same time very exciting. I soon became just as abandoned as he. But beginning a few months ago, he has become more "stable." He says now that we're approaching marriage, we should begin acting like a mature, grown-up couple—which seems to mean one position only. He tells me "childish kicks" are unnecessary in an adult marital relationship—but after three years of "kicks" this monotonous idea is too much for me to take. If his attitude makes him a "mature" 24-year-old, then I prefer to stay immature. I love and need everything we've had before and this new "stability" is impossible for me to adjust to. We're slowly drifting apart. Now I am the most frustrated female in California—and it's the old him that I want. I hope this is only a passing fancy with him—if it isn't, we cannot possibly marry. He says it's up to me to change and claims I'm oversexed and need to visit a doctor. He says that if the next three years were like the last three, it would kill him. But what we have now is killing me. Please help.—Miss A. K., Palo Alto, California.

We think you're confusing the nuptial mattress with a gymnasium mat. Your fiancé will wear himself to a frazzle—mentally as well as physically—if you insist that he spend most of his waking hours trying to top his last act. We suspect that his declining sexual interest, and your ever-increasing demands, are both symptomatic of a deeper dissatisfaction—on whose part we can't say. We suggest a long talk—face to face, both seated—to determine what the trouble is. Depending on the result, you must be ready to consider breaking your engagement. However, if he really is just pooped (and we don't for a minute discount the possibility), then you might be able to hit on an agreeable compromise somewhere between acrobatics and monotony.

My girlfriend, who is a prude, thinks it's scandalous that I don't wear any underwear. I say it's my business. Who's right?—K. L., Juneau, Alaska.

It's your business all right, but how do you keep warm during those six-month winters they've got up there? And if your girl's a prude, how'd she find out?

What can you do about a girl who wants to know everything about your past sex life? I'm dating a sweet young chick who is very liberal-minded about such things—she says there must be no secrets between us, and that unless she knows all about my past affairs she can't possibly enter into a mature and understanding relationship. But I'm damned if I want to air my past escapades, either for her or for anyone else. How can I cope?—F. D., Louisville, Kentucky.

Your past haymaking is definitely your own concern, and should remain so. We suggest you be doubly gallant: gallant to your past inamoratas by protecting their names and reputations, and gallant to your present girl by telling her that your past pales into insignificance when compared with your current feelings toward her and your expectations of mutual gratification. You should also make it abundantly clear that you're not interested in her past, since you feel it's none of your business. If she doesn't dig the vice versa application of this, the evidence would seem to indicate that her interest in you is too sick to produce the mature and understanding relationship she's dangling.

The girl with whom I am currently engaged (physically, that is) insists on being in complete charge whenever we become intimate. The first time we dated, I was rewarded with an unbuttoned blouse (not of my doing) after only a few kisses. But on the next date, when I went for the buttons, I was set back with a stern: "If you want me undressed, I'll do it myself." Is she suffering from some psychological disorder or is she simply overly helpful? Any suggestions?—B. W., Des Moines, Iowa.

If her dominating attitude makes you uncomfortable it might be well for you to zip out of the relationship. Sex, at its best, should be spontaneous—with no "rules" inhibiting either partner. If your girl's desire to take the lead shows up in other ways as well, chances are her psyche requires her to undo her beaux as well as her buttons.

I've been a widow for two of my 26 years, and during that time I've encountered a problem which I hope your sage advice will solve. My job as secretary to a junior exec permits me to meet many men of all types. But since I'm not interested in remarriage, nor a free meal and an evening's entertainment, I accept dates with only those for whom I feel a reasonably strong attraction at the moment. Now, I have no intention of becoming promiscuous, but neither do I intend to say "No" to anyone to whom I'm physically attracted. Apparently, I'm attractive, too, since the men in my life these past two years insist that I am about the best thing on which they have ever laid eyes. But now, something has begun to work on my subconscious and is making me doubtful of my femininity: I have two disturbing figure faults—breasts that lack the firmness and youthful look of the lovely girls within your pages, and stretch marks on my hips. None of my sexual partners has ever mentioned these as deterrents, but can you cosmopolitan men-about-town tell me if most men *do* feel repulsed by such less-than-perfect attributes? Help!—S. C., Boston, Massachusetts.

Fret not. Femininity is far more a matter of attitude than anatomy and no male worth his salt expects perfection in either department; men are going to like you for what you are, and, judging from your letter, that's quite a bit.

Every night I dream that I am being married to Brigitte Bardot, but at the very moment I kiss her, I wake up. I am losing much sleep in this fashion.— R. O., Victoria, Australia.

A sleeping pill or two should see you on through the ceremony and into the bridal suite. Happy honeymoon!

My girl and I have a really great thing going, with one exception: She's as demanding as she is affectionate, and constantly wants to hear little endearments from me. We've talked about it, and she says she just enjoys a constant stream of love talk. Not long ago I got disgusted with this state of affairs and clammed up, until her irritation approached tantrum level. I'm beginning to feel like a stuck record, and wonder if you can help me out of this groove. (Please don't give me your "dump her" line. I'm genuinely fond of this girl, and want to maintain our otherwise blissful relationship.)—G. A., Detroit, Michigan.

You're just going to have to take the bitter with the sweet—and taking the bitter in this case means

*giving the sweets. Your options are quite clear: You
can either satisfy her appetite for endearment, deny
it and endure the tantrums that follow, or (your ad-
monition notwithstanding) dump her.*

How can I explain to overinquisitive male drinking
companions that I have no taste for bull-session bel-
lowing about my rather peripatetic but nevertheless
private sex life?—R. H., Los Angeles, California.

*You might try a sermon about the immaturity of
vicarious sexual experience, or even point out that
authorities are in general agreement that such sharing
has homosexual undertones—if you don't mind losing
friends. But if you want to keep your drinking buddies, we suggest the following: surfeit them with the
most wildly implausible situations you can concoct;
toss in everything from Frank Harris to Sacher-
Masoch; be unstinting in your attention to detail;
embroider an erotic pastiche that will pop their eyes.
You will be much admired for your Rabelaisian tale-
telling; when your bar buddies sheepishly discover that
they have been beautifully put on, they will be more
than content to let you keep your own counsel.*

What can you do about a girl who insists that all
her lovemaking be done according to an established
routine? The girl I refer to has a warm and winning
personality and I am very fond of her. But if I want
to express my affection in the most fundamental way,
I must first work through a three- or four-hour ob-
stacle course: First she's got to have a leisurely dinner
by candlelight. Then a session of cheek-to-cheek

dancing in her or my apartment. At which point—if my small talk has been sufficiently romantic—it is finally possible to take her hand and lead her into the next room for the reaping of greater rewards (an activity she undertakes with authentic enthusiasm). Having gone this route several times by now, I find the prefatory performance increasingly ridiculous— and I have told her so. She says that far from being silly these preliminaries are absolutely essential to her —that without the soft lights and music and romantic murmurings she just can't get in the mood. To me, this bit—as a regimented and unvarying routine— loses all meaning. Do you think I'm being selfish in wanting to inject some spontaneity into the picture? —J. W., Washington, D.C.

Not at all. The girl obviously has some phychological roadblocks in her sex drive that should be removed forthwith. This can perhaps best be achieved by demonstrating to her that there is as much, if not more, joy to be had from spontaneous combustion as from an elaborately prepared fire. Choose a moment far removed from your habitual nighttime setting—after Sunday breakfast, say, or during an afternoon drive in the country—and proceed with persuasive ardor to try to bring her to terms. There's a good chance that her defense mechanisms will crumble, and that she'll soon be thanking you for having liberated her libido.

Lately I've been seeing a girl whose sexual desires seem almost insatiable. Certainly, sex is a nice way to conclude an evening, but this girl often likes it to begin a date as well as end it—and on a few occasions she's actually requested that we cut short a night on the town and slip back to my pad for a refresher. At first I found her avidity personally flattering; but now I'm wondering if it might be more than just me. Tell me: Just when does a highly sexed girl qualify as a nymphomaniac?—L. S., Washington, D.C.

Nymphomania is less a matter of sexual frequency than an insatiable female craving for coitus for pathological, rather than sexual, reasons; true nymphomania is rare, and we doubt that it's your, or your girl's, problem. Normal sexual desire varies considerably from one person to another, in both men and women; but if your girl requires sexual gratification twice or more an evening as a steady diet, her need may be more emotional than physical. However, unless she seems in other ways unhappy or unstable, you probably don't need to be concerned for her psychological well-being. Your own physical well-being is something else again; perhaps a little more bed rest and some vitamins will put you in tune. And, lest what should be pleasure turn into drudgery, don't hesitate to discuss your concern with her.

Every time I get down to basics with my girl she insists that our affection find its deepest expression in pitch darkness. Since I personally would prefer to have at least one light on, these pleas for complete obscurity are beginning to bug me. I mean, is there something basically wrong with having a bit of illumination? Or is there perhaps something wrong with her?—O. T., Philadelphia, Pennsylvania.

Your attitude is entirely normal—as is hers. According to Kinsey, "In general, more men prefer to have intercourse in the light and more women prefer it in the dark." Patient persuasion on your part should lead to a brighter tomorrow.

I'm a medical student doing night hospital duty. Last night I had the opportunity to initiate a promising relationship with a student nurse—in a vacant hospital room. (Many more things go on in a hospital than meet the public eye.) Unhappily, we were caught in a very compromising situation by the night head nurse. After she told my Nightingale to fly off, I was expecting a first-degree dressing down—and instead got a proposition. She told me she'd be willing to forget the whole thing if only I'd come over to her apartment one day soon "to talk things over." She's quite attractive, in her late 20s, and I'd gladly do whatever is necessary to atone for my misdeed. But the situation is clouded by the fact that her husband (they're physically but not legally separated) lives in the same neighborhood. If he barged in, I'd be in a bigger mess than I'm in now. What's the solution?— J. K., New York, New York.

The long-range solution is for you to stop improvising bedrooms and get your own. The immediate solution is for you to keep away from Mrs. Head Nurse, and hope that she'll forget both that she surprised you flagrante delicto, and that she attempted to blackmail you into making love to her. Her role in this affair has been as indiscreet as yours—a conclusion that she herself will certainly reach before she ever thinks seriously about reporting you. Count yourself lucky this time, and hereafter save your bedside manner for off-duty bedsides.

Is it proper to remove a girl's fashion wig before making love to her?—S. L., Baltimore, Maryland.

When making love on relatively formal (black-tie) occasions, leave your partner wigged. On informal dates, country weekends, and any time before five, untressing is permissible—if your date consents, of course. But under no circumstances should you move to remove your partner's wig if you suspect (1) she's not wearing one, or (2) she's bald underneath.

■'m currently going with a girl whose company I enjoy considerably. We have a good relationship going on all levels, except for one thing: I can't get this girl to share a bed with me. She's perfectly compliant —even aggressive—on my living-room couch, or in a parked auto, or other places you'd hardly call romantic. But whenever I mention the word "bed" she freezes. I'd like you to tell me how to get her bedded down, as I'm about ready for the chiropractor.— F. A., Louisville, Kentucky.

Your girl needs a rationalization for every sexual contact ("We were talking on the couch and just got carried away"). You might try to solve the problem by discussing the matter with her in a good-natured way, pointing out that while her idiosyncrasy has little effect on her sex life, it may be seriously endangering her posture; or you can try to crash the barrier, by getting a convertible couch or calling on the persuasive powers of passion to lead her to your bower. In either case, after your initial featherbedding, subsequent sojourns to the Simmons should be no problem.

■ have been going out with a psychiatrist for two months. I went to bed with him for the first time a week ago—and since then, not one word from him. (All right, I don't expect Lawrence Welk serenading me beneath my window the morning after or any little mementos from Tiffany's, but don't you think I'm justified in expecting at least one call?) Is there any way I could call him without making a complete fool of myself, or do all you men of the world think I should just accept the fact that he found the whole experience unsatisfactory and decided to cross me out of his little black book? I must admit, I'm not the world's most exciting creature, but no one has complained before.—C. B., New Orleans, Louisiana.

Since no one has complained before, relax. Your erstwhile headshrinker may be the kind who enjoys the chase more than the trophy. If so, that's his hang-up, not yours. Don't bug him with phone calls, but you might drop him a note recommending he see a good psychiatrist.

My friends and I have had a slight disagreement over the frequency with which a normal male can achieve satisfaction in one night. I've heard cohorts boast of amazing physical powers, and I've often thought that perhaps I fall short. Try as I may, I can only experience seven orgasms, and then must quit because of physical exhaustion, even though my partner is willing and able to continue research. Should I take a body-building course?—L. N., San Francisco, California.

Take one? You should be giving one.

Not too long ago, through a peculiar turn of events which I won't go into, I came upon my girl's diary, and was astonished to see that she had outlined—and in the minutest detail—our sexual activities. In fact, thumbing through, I saw that the book contained very little else besides such descriptions. I'm at a loss to decide how I should respond to this peculiarity. Should I pretend I never saw this book? Should I tell her to stop making entries? Or to destroy it?—W. T., Newport News, Virginia.

Better just forget you ever saw the book. If you discuss the matter with your girl, you'll have to admit you've been perusing her personal property—and that's far stickier than her clinical recording of your amours. You should find some gratification in the knowledge that she thinks enough of your love-making to want to retain the details—though we generally disapprove of this sort of thing, since the diary could be a problem if it happened to fall into the wrong hands.

One of the girls I date is perfectly normal with one exception: She insists that we each take a hot, soapy shower immediately after intercourse. I don't particularly mind this, but it has a ritual air which I find a little eerie. Do you?—K. C., Walla Walla, Washington.

Yes, but if these hygienic high jinks are the only hang-up in an otherwise good relationship, count yourself lucky (and clean).

How often does a man of 28 require sex? My husband makes love to me only once every 10 to 14 days and I think that two to three times a week is closer to normal. We've been married four years and I am now 21. He insists that I'm oversexed, that he's normal and that "married life isn't only sex." Which of us requires medical help? If it is he and he refuses to seek help, should I have an affair—which is against my beliefs—or should I seek a divorce? One thing more: he has gone out with other women and every time he does he later accuses me of having cheated, too.—J. N., Denver, Colorado.

Sexual frequency varies greatly from man to man and couple to couple, but two to three times a week is considered the average for couples in their 20s. Of course, marriage isn't all sex, as your husband says, but certainly you deserve all he has to offer in that area. Since this sort of dilemma is seldom one-sided, we suggest that both of you check with your friendly neighborhood marriage counselor.

So much emphasis is placed on the complexities of sex today that people frequently don't learn the fundamentals. Like me, for example, I'm a girl in her early 20s who knows her way around a boudoir but has never learned to kiss properly. At least, I don't think I have. When I'm in the early stages of amour, I worry so much about osculation etiquette that I don't enjoy myself. *Please:* How long do you hold a kiss? Who breaks first, guy or girl? Is it OK to breathe while kissing? Is kissing a fundamental part of marriage? How many kisses should transpire before you move on to other things?—Miss A. L., Wichita, Kansas.

How long you hold a kiss is optional. If you're a farm girl, you might "Kiss till the cow comes home," as suggested by the 17th Century playwrights Beaumont and Fletcher. Break time can be initiated by either sex. Breath-holding during osculation is more common to grade-B Hollywood films of the Thirties (the kind where the hero says to the girl, "You poor little thing, you're trembling") than to real life: Unless you relish turning blue, keep your nose functioning. Marriages are made up of different fundamental parts; novelist George Meredith (whose married life, it should be noted, was singularly unsuccessful) commented: "Kissing don't last; cookery do!" No one can answer your last question but yourself.

In recent months I've been dating three girls whose first names all begin with J. Though in vertical moments I have no difficulty remembering the right name, the intoxication of love-making often implants a mix-up in my sweet nothings. This is far from a frivolous question, as the problem has ruined more than one evening for me and still persists. Can you help?— A. R., Cleveland, Ohio.

Select an endearing euphemism applicable to all, along the lines of "Angel" or "Kitten." Use this constantly for all hands and you never need fear miss misnomers.

My girl insists I keep my eyes closed during any serious kissing. I see nothing wrong in going into things with my eyes wide open. Who's correct?— R. J., Wantagh, New York.

To look or not to look is purely a matter of personal taste. However, when your partner adamantly insists that you assume any particular attitude, chances are it bespeaks something amiss in her own. If it's just a whim, why not humor her? Or perhaps she'll settle for one eye?

Is there any way to be sure of getting a hotel room or motel room with a double bed instead of twin beds? It embarrasses me to ask for a double, but worse, it sometimes cools off my companion.—W. F., New Orleans, Louisiana.

Easiest way is to make reservations in advance, requesting a double. No cause for embarrassment, but if you're the shy type write or wire. You sure as hell won't embarrass the reservations clerk no matter how you do it.

The girl I go with has a problem. She can't get interested in sex until after she's roared up and down the highway for an hour at the wheel of my car (or hers) at speeds in excess of 100 mph. I say she should become aroused in a more normal fashion (even the swankiest dine-and-drink date leaves her cold if it's not capped with one of these joy rides), but she says fast driving is kicksville for her. I am becoming especially concerned because she is not a very good driver, though she has yet to have a wreck.—C. L., Brockton, Massachusetts.

Kicksville? That's more like grimreapersville. Unless she gets some psychiatric help in a hurry, you're both heading for trouble.

Being a ski instructor, I get to meet different young women every week. The girls I teach are usually pretty, if not beautiful, and most of them wear very expensive, sexy outfits that apparently give an excellent idea of the wearer's structure—or so I thought. The sad fact is that when I have gotten together with some of them, in the wee hours of the morning, I have more than once found to my surprise that I have been cheated—that is, nature had been improved upon by some strategically positioned upholstery. My question involves the proper etiquette when confronted with such a discovery. Do I ignore it, or do I have the right to be angry?—B. H., Stowe, Vermont.

Ignore it. It's as natural and proper for a flat-chested girl to put up a false front as it is to wear lipstick and eye make-up. You wouldn't want to spend time with a girl who didn't think enough of herself to try to be as attractively dressed as possible, would you? We once heard of a popular movie queen who even had falsies sewn into her nightgowns, but that, of course, is carrying things a bit too far. Hide your disappointment and enjoy. After all, the proof's not in the padding, but in the performance.

If you can top this one—or even answer it—I'll buy a lifetime subscription to PLAYBOY at once. The other night I had a date with a real swinging girlfriend with whom I've had a totally satisfying relationship. That is, we like each other hugely, get on beautifully, are uninhibited about doing what comes naturally, freely date others (and never discuss it afterward), yet each of us knows and doesn't care that it's not for keeps and no strings will be left dangling.

As I said, the other night I had a date with her and it went like so: I called for her at her apartment, found a note to me hung on her doorbell saying her mother (who lives out of the city and whom I'd never met) was upstairs, that she (the girl) had had a command-performance, last-minute dinner invite from her boss to dine with an important client, and that I should go

on up and have a drink with the old lady and wait
for my girl to get back if I wished. Up I went and
used the bell, not my key, and got the surprise of
my life. This mother is like no mother you ever saw—
very youthful, full of magnetism, zing and charm,
and downright beautiful. She must be in her 30s, but
looks like 25. Her 18-year-old daughter takes after
her, but it's Mom who has the looks and the sophisti-
cation to a degree that makes her daughter seem a dim
carbon copy by comparison.

Mom and I got on great, had some drinks, talked
a lot. I swear I could feel the electric tension building up between us, and I didn't know what to do, so
I asked her to come on out for something to eat. We
went to an Italian restaurant (candles and chianti)
and I was pretty sure this wonderful hunk of woman
was feeling the way I did. I tested it by asking her to
the pad I share with my bachelor dad (who wasn't
due home that night) for a brandy, she accepted, and
—as it turned out pretty quickly—my hunch was right.
In fact, we had a torrid session compared to which
my previous experience, which I thought was exten-
sive, is kid stuff. Along about three A.M., we sort of
came to and I took her back to her daughter's pad.
I figured it would be best not to wake the girl—assuming she was asleep—and her mother agreed, so
I used my key, the idea being that her mother would
tiptoe to bed and tell her in the morning that I'd decided not to wait. Boy, did I get a shock when I
opened that front door! There, on the bearskin rug
before the dying embers in the fireplace was *my* girl,
in her birthday suit, sound asleep in the arms of my
snoring dad, who was similarly dressed. Our entrance
woke them, there was a moment of stunned embarrassment, then we all started talking at once, ac-
cusing each other of every breach of faith and pro-

priety, raising our voices, threatening, et cetera. I gave up at last and just split and went to a hotel, where I now sit writing this. What to do now?—L. G., New York, New York.

You are too talented a fellow to be wasting such fiction on a magazine column that doesn't pay any money. Of course, your imaginary tale is a bit too cliché-ridden for the slick market—at least without some additional embellishments—but it sounds as though it might be just the thing for one of the sex magazines, and you may be able to earn enough from it to pay that $150 for the Lifetime Subscription you owe us.

This may seem an inconsequential thing to you, but my boyfriend, Dud, whistles when he makes love to me. What's he up to?—K. H., Augusta, Maine.

Assuming he's not just whistling "Dixie," it all depends on the tune. (And with a name like Dud, you're lucky he doesn't just lie there.) If his routine is no more complicated than a few rounds of, say, "Heart-aches," then he probably thinks he's being romantic. However, if he gets involved in more complicated works (Bach's "Chromatic Fantasy and Fugue" or Stravinsky's "Le Sacre du Printemps"), then he might be practicing for a night-club act—and a pretty good one at that. Of course, if he's whistling at other girls, you'd best ask them to leave the room.